A PROSPECTUS FOR THE TRIUMPH OF REALISM

A PROSPECTUS FOR THE TRIUMPH OF REALISM

Thomas A. Russman

MERCER
UNIVERSITY PRESS

ISBN 0-86554-232-5

A Prospectus for the Triumph of Realism

Mercer University Press, Macon GA 31207

Printed in the United States of America

The paper used in this publication meets the minimum requirements of American National Standard for Information Sciences—Permanence of Paper for Printed Library Materials, ANSI Z39.48-1984.

Library of Congress Cataloging-in-Publication Data

Russman, Thomas A.
A prospectus for the triumph of realism.

Includes index.
1. Philosophy. 2. Realism. I. Title.
B53.R87 1987 149'.2 86-28646
ISBN 0-86554-232-5

CONTENTS

PREFACE

Anyone who pursues an M.A. in philosophy from The Catholic University of America and a Ph.D. in philosophy from Princeton University probably is asking for trouble. My M.A. director was William Wallace and my Ph.D. director Richard Rorty. This book is the eventual result of that cross-pollination.

The history of philosophy does not continually repeat itself, but it does continually return to familiar ground in new ways. Views "definitively put aside" return later, once the uncomfortable consequences of their too complete rejection have been played out. Not that "comfort" or "discomfort" is or ought to be the ultimate standard. But discomfort with established views can at least motivate a resourceful reexamination.

Simply stated, my purpose is to return in a new way to the once familiar ground of epistemological realism—the pre-Cartesian view that things-themselves are knowable through perception and that such knowledge is foundational. My understanding of the traps that lie in my path has been greatly enlightened by the work of such recent antifoundationalists as Wilfrid Sellars, Willard Quine, Thomas Kuhn, and, of course, Richard Rorty. The views of these philosophers also constitute the strongest contemporary source of my philosophical discomfort.

This new way of realism I call "informal foundationalism." Other writers (Fred Dretske, Rom Harré, Karl Popper, to name very few) have been at work on parts of a contemporary realism for some time. My rather comprehensive version requires me to defend "givenness" at the observation level and to resuscitate the theory/observation distinction, while saving all there is of hard evidence for recent views to the contrary. This effort provides my central arguments and occupies most of the first seven chapters.

Doing this much does not seem to me enough, however, if we are to lay out, in at least a preliminary way, the main issues that divide foundationalists from their opponents. Some of these issues are broadly moral, political, and cultural. A book three times the length of this one could not explore the further issues fully, and such a book would be likely to lose focus as it gained completeness. The alternatives were either to omit the broader discussions entirely or to give them a relatively brief and somewhat programmatic treatment. The latter was the path finally chosen. I leave to the reader's judgment whether the final chapters (8-12) of this "prospectus" justify that choice.

The word "triumph" in the title—even though somewhat attenuated by the word "prospectus"—is, no doubt, a bit inflated. It seems clear that, even if realism becomes generally acknowledged as a viable philosophical alternative, other philosophical views will continue to have intelligent, nay, brilliant, champions. Perhaps I express only a complacent prejudice when I speculate that most people would really rather be realists, once they see their way clear. If this prejudice happens to be correct, and if the way can indeed be cleared, then the "prospect" for some sort of "triumph" may, to that extent, be real enough.

Betty Adam offered useful advice and assurances concerning chapter 11. Claire Hill did the same for chapter 12. The faculty at the Center for Thomistic Studies afforded me excellent discussions of the body/soul relationship in Aristotle and Aquinas. Eileen Powers typed and edited the early draft. An anonymous reader for Mercer University Press was uncommonly careful and exact in his criticisms and suggestions. What I did with all this helpfulness is, of course, my own responsibility.

Chapter I

THE MYTH OF THE FRAMEWORK

In his lively criticism of Thomas Kuhn in the mid-1960s, Karl Popper attacked what he called "the myth of the framework."[1] According to this myth there is no neutral ground upon which to discuss or compare the frameworks of competing scientific theories. They can only be discussed or compared from within one of the competing frameworks. Thus a Copernican cosmologist could compare his own views with those of a Ptolemaic cosmologist, but he would do so only from the vantage point of his own views, using them as a standard against which to measure the merits and demerits of Ptolemy. Of course, the Ptolemaic cosmologist could to the same thing, if he cared to, subjecting Copernicus to the standard of Ptolemy. A theorist with a third point of view could offer to arbitrate. But then he would only be applying the standard of his own theory to the other two theories. And so an Einsteinian cosmologist would discuss the relative merits of Ptolemy and Copernicus in terms of their resemblance to Einstein. According to the myth of the framework, the well educated, late-twentieth-century reader thinks Ptolemaic theory inferior to Copernican and Einsteinean because, by training, he is Copernican and Einsteinian. The progress of science is just our Whiggish

[1]Karl Popper, "Normal Science and Its Dangers," in Imre Lakotos and Alan Musgrave, eds., *Criticism and the Growth of Knowledge* (London: Cambridge University Press, 1970) 56.

resume of the history of science interpreted so as to lead dramatically to the views generally held today.

As Kuhn himself described it, Karl Popper's fundamental disagreement with the myth of the framework is his assumption "that theories can be compared by recourse to a basic vocabulary consisting entirely of words which are attached to nature in ways that are . . . to the extent necessary, independent of theory."[2] Kuhn denied that such a neutral observation vocabulary exists. It is not hard to understand Kuhn's point. Suppose two physicists are looking at a cloud chamber photo. One claims that the photo shows a zigging positron. The other claims the photo shows a zagging electron. As chance would have it, each is claiming to see that which confirms his own competing theory. This is the sort of thing Kuhn has in mind when he denies that there is a neutral observation language. The observation language takes on the color of the observer's theory.

Kuhn's point is clear, but it does not disprove the existence of Popper's neutral observation language. Granted that "zigging positron" and "zagging electron" are not, in the case cited, examples of neutral observation language, the two physicists can easily unburden their observation language of these question-begging terms. Then they might get down to something less technical and quite neutral, like "right-swerving squiggle." In other words, regardless of their theoretical bias, both physicists are seeing the same squiggle on the photograph and can describe it in language neutral to their competing theories. We would not expect one to say the squiggle went left while the other says it went right just because they hold different theories. Nor would we expect one to describe a right-angle change of course while the other describes a sweeping arc, just so each can defend his own theory. There is always a neutral observation language available, lying under the biased one. We can always move to the commonsense observation language and leave the peculiar language of the competing theories behind. Popper was right to insist that this neutral observation language exists and is always available.

The trouble is that, as the cloud chamber example shows, what can be said in the neutral observation language is so often undecisive for theory choice. Both physicists see the squiggle, but both theories predicted the same sort of squiggle. And so, nothing is

---

[2]Thomas S. Kuhn, "Reflections on My Critics," ibid., 266.

decided. Kuhn was right to emphasize this point, but Popper had no reason to disagree with it. All competing theories have a vast underlay of identical predictions in the neutral observation language. If they did not, they would not have reached the status of theories in the first place. Obviously, if we are looking for ways to decide between theories, we must look elsewhere. Not all competing predictions in the neutral observation language are identical. The shape of the orbit of Mercury confirmed Einsteinian predictions and contradicted Newtonian predictions. Newtonians did not try to claim that their readings of Mercury's orbit were different. The vocabulary of these readings was neutral with regard to the theories being compared. The chemical analysis of the moon rocks confirmed some predictions and disconfirmed others. Laboratory results did not differ according to the theories of the technicians producing them. The vocabulary of chemical analysis was neutral to the theories being compared, as was the observation language used to make the analysis.

In summary, there is a neutral observation language for use in comparing theories. Two competing theories will always have many common predictions in the neutral observation language. There can be significantly different predictions, however, and the results for or against can be undeniable and undeniably neutral.

Kuhn was right, however, to insist that there are other factors that figure in theory comparison/choice and that often enough these other factors have a decisive role to play. Simplicity is one such factor. We make use of scientific theories to predict what will happen and to organize our data. If a simpler theory does this as well as a more complex one, we will naturally favor the simpler one with its simpler calculations. In contexts where such instrumentalist concerns are paramount, a simpler theory may be preferred even when it is less well confirmed by observation than its alternative. Suppose theory A and theory B are equally successful predictors within a restricted range of phenomena. Suppose A is simpler than B, but B is a more successful predictor beyond this restricted range of phenomena. It will not be surprising if researchers interested only in the restricted range prefer A to B. Even the scientific realist must admit that instrumentality has its point.

The realism of the theories being compared is another factor in theory choice, and this is where the scientific realist makes *his* point. Scientists are not only interested in supplying themselves with instruments for prediction and data organization. They want to say not only that given a, b will follow—but also *why* it will follow. Scientists are therefore committed to supplying explanatory models that portray plausible underlying mechanisms to tell us why certain phenomena appear together. Scientists prefer one theory to another if the model of the underlying mechanisms is more "realistic." Some theories make barely a stab at describing plausible underlying mechanisms. Ptolemaic epicycles can, in principle, be made sufficiently complex to save all the appearances and make all the right predictions. But why are the planets darting around the sky in this irregular fashion? A mechanism described in terms of gravitational force and relative motion eventually came to the support of Copernicus' theoretical descendants. This mechanism, however incompletely understood, made Ptolemaic epicycles less desirable on grounds of realism as well as on grounds of simplicity. The more realistic model is preferred because it offers a more satisfactory answer to the "why questions" scientists perpetually ask.

Models can be judged unrealistic not only when they fail to offer underlying mechanisms, but also when the mechanisms they offer are incoherent or conflict with mechanisms described in other well confirmed theories. A model would be incoherent and, to that extent, unrealistic, if it required the same particle to be in two places at the same time or to be spinning in contrary directions at the same time. The wave and particle theories of light have never been adequately synthesized and remain unsatisfactory from a realistic point of view. They give theoretically incompatible answers to "why questions" about light. But in this case no more realistic alternative to our present theories has been offered; and so, despite the "unrealism," these theories continue to be fruitfully used. Realism in theories is an important scientific ideal and an important factor in theory choice; but when it fails to be decisive, instrumental considerations can take up enough slack to keep unrealistic theories in use indefinitely.

Karl Popper had his own way of emphasizing the importance of a theory's claim to be real or true. Suppose, he reasoned, we have a theory that generates novel predictions of phenomena never before observed or measured, predictions that we would have no reason to expect except for this theory. Now suppose these novel predictions are confirmed. Popper argued that it is highly improbable that such dramatic success is the result of mere chance. Such success gives us very powerful grounds for believing that the mechanisms modeled by the theory dramatically approach the truth about the world.[3] And so, for Popper, the realism of a theory is most powerfully witnessed only by a dramatic return to neutral observation through the testing of novel predictions.

Here finally we have found what was the central point of disagreement between Popper and Kuhn. It was not, as Kuhn thought, that Popper believed in an observation language standing neutral between scientific theories; for Kuhn should admit that such a language does exist and can be discovered in every case of theory comparison or choice. Nor was it Kuhn's insistence that simplicity, coherence, and other factors also have their place in theory comparison/choice; Popper cheerfully admits that they do. The issue that divides them is whether the observation language is merely neutral as between two competing scientific theories, or whether it is neutral in a far more radical sense. Does our observation language offer a primary, truthful access to the world as it is in itself? The whole force of Popper's procedure for claiming truth by verified novel predictions depends upon the assumption that it does. According to this procedure, the truth of our scientific (and other) theories must be checked through the unique access offered by observation. When theories pass this test, not only by being designed to explain antecedently observed connections, but also by anticipating new connections via novel predictions, they participate in the truthful access of observation and carry it deeper.

But does our observation framework give us this sort of special access to permanent truths about the world? If it does, then the myth of the framework is routed, for observation gives us a way into frameworks and out of them. But if it does not, then despite all that was granted above concerning a neutral observation language, the myth of the framework is still flying high and going strong. An observation framework that is neutral with regard to competing scientific theories might nevertheless be replaceable itself, just as they are. In that case the observation framework could itself be ultimately regarded as just another competing framework, albeit the most ancient and familiar one (and therefore heir to some sense of privilege). But then the observation language is plainly not the abode of permanent truths about the world, and we must be open to the possibility that our scientific frameworks

---

[3]Karl Popper, *Conjectures and Refutations* (New York: Harper, 1965) 242ff. Popper lists "successful novel predictions" as the third requirement for the growth of scientific knowledge.

may at some point require us to correct any part of our observational beliefs. In other words it will be okay for us to decide to make the standards of some scientific theory preeminent, even if by that standard our traditional observation framework is contradicted. Just such a situation is what Popper saw as the sway of the myth of the framework.

The battle between the myth of the framework and what Wilfrid Sellars called "the myth of the given" is a battle to death. Either something in the observation framework is permanently given (myth of the given) or the observation framework, like all other frameworks, is subject to rejection at the hands of competing frameworks (myth of the framework). When I referred to the "Triumph of Realism" in the title of this book, I was referring to realism about the observation framework: the view that it is the abode of permanent truths about the world. It will be my aim to show that what Sellars called the myth of the given is actually right when applied to observation. I am quite aware that this opinion is out of vogue. But if, as I think I can show, the vogue is wrong, it will be interesting to understand why the vogue arose.

The next step is to examine Sellars's attack upon the myth of the given, and particularly the assumptions about perception and language that propel it.

Chapter II

THE MYTH OF THE GIVEN

Wilfrid Sellars is a wholehearted disciple of the myth of the framework, at least as it applies to observation. He not only denies that in principle the observation framework as we now have it is given, he claims that we can *already see that it is false.*[1] It is false, says Sellars, because it contradicts the scientific framework; and, given a choice between the two, we ought reasonably to choose the scientific framework because of its greater explanatory power.[2] The appeal to explanatory power is not an appeal to a neutral standard, it is just the standard of the scientific framework itself as Sellars construes it. Sellars thinks we have by now become sufficiently imbued with the scientific framework that we are ready to call the observation framework into question in its name. He then attempts to show us why and how we should do so.[3]

Sellars's apologetic for the myth of the framework begins with his well-known attack on "the myth of the given." Sellars as-

---

[1]Wilfrid Sellars, *Science, Perception and Reality* (New York: Humanities Press, 1963) 126.

[2]Wilfrid Sellars, "Science, Sense Impressions, and Sensa," *Review of Metaphysics* 23:3 (March 1970): 429.

[3]I have discussed Sellars's hows and whys elsewhere and have argued that they do not work: Thomas A. Russman, "The Problem of the Two Images," in Joseph Pitt, ed., *The Philosophy of Wilfrid Sellars: Queries and Extensions* (Boston: D. Reidel, 1978) 73-103.

sumes throughout this attack that there is no such thing as nonconceptual (or preconceptual) perceptual awareness. He assumes this, he does not argue for it. It is this assumption that unravels his attack, as we shall see.

James Cornman was one of the few who recognized this assumption for the bare thing that it is. Cornman believed that perceptual experience—whether in humans or other animals—involves sensing, that is, a state of awareness, "and this occurs in those perceivers who do not have any concepts whatsoever."[4] Sellars contradicts this, saying, "Such experiencing essentially involves a conceptual act."[5] Cornman restates Sellars's assumption: "Each state of *s* experiencing the property, redness, is a conceptual state of s."[6] Cornman searches Sellars's writings for any reason to accept this assumption. He finds none. He wonders what would oblige us to say that infants and other animals, having sensory apparatus very similar to our own, nevertheless lack sensory awareness, simply because they lack concepts. I will state Cornman's point more sharply: unless Sellars gives us strong reasons to deny the existence of nonconceptual awareness, the sensory apparatus and behavior of many nonconceptual creatures, being so much like our own, should persuade us that they are indeed aware.

Now let's turn specifically to Sellars's attack upon the myth of the given. At the start I will be interested to show two things: (1) the attack assumes that nonconceptual awareness does not exist; (2) the attack does not support this assumption, though it might appear to do so.

Sellars claims that "the abstractive theory" of concept formation "makes the mistake of supposing that the logical space of the concept simply transfers itself from the objects of direct perception to the intellectual order, or better, is transferred by the mind as Jack Horner transferred the plum."[7] Sellars's complaint is quite understandable. Concepts cannot come to us as isolated little plums of meaning. An infant cannot, by gazing on a plum, extract the solitary concept "plum" from it. This concept depends for its meaning upon relations to other concepts, like

---

[4]James Cornman, "Sellarsian Scientific Realism without Sensa," ibid., 69.

[5]Quoted by Cornman, ibid.

[6]Ibid.

[7]Sellars, *Science, Perception and Reality, 90.*

"fruit," "eat," "round," "red," and so forth. A child cannot have just one concept; it must have many or none at all. This is true of all concepts common to, say, most English-speakers. But it would also be true of more primitive languages that we might speculate were the prehistoric ancestors of languages alive today. It seems reasonable to assume that some of these primitive languages were limited to highly ostensive uses, to identifying and asking for particular concrete items. But Wittgenstein was right to point out that concepts in even such primitive languages (as described in his *Philosophical Investigations,* #2) are related to one another by rules for their correct use and are thus part of a larger framework or language game. This fact refutes any theory of concept formation that claims concepts are given one at a time, to be strung together later into frameworks. Sellars and I set such givens aside as indefensible.

The myth of the given seems to involve more than "plum concepts," however, and to come in many forms. "But," says Sellars, "they all have in common the idea that the awareness of certain *sorts* . . . is a primordial, non-problematic feature of 'immediate experience.' "[8] What is a "sort?" "(B)y 'sorts' I have in mind, in the first instance, determinate sense repeatables."[9] What is a "determinate sense repeatable?" Sellars's ensuing discussion makes clear that a determinate sense repeatable is a particular perceived *as* the sort of thing that it is. I am aware of a "sort" when I am aware of a red ball *as* red or *as* a ball or *as* both. The theory of concept formation Sellars is attacking holds that we develop the concepts "ball," "red," "round" in a process that begins by perceiving things *as* balls, *as* red, and *as* round and eliciting the concepts from such perceptions. But such original perceptions are problematic, says Sellars. To perceive something *as* red requires that one already be using the concept "red" to perceive it so. One does not *develop* the concept from such perception; the concept is already presupposed by such perception. Nor is it any help, says Sellars, to try to start the process a step further back by saying that before one sees red as red, one sees one red thing as similar to another red thing. To see one thing as similar to another, one needs to have concepts like "similar." In an effort to show how concepts are developed from perceptions of "sorts," we have only man-

[8]Ibid., 157.

[9]Ibid.

aged to show that concepts are presupposed by perceptions of "sorts." This line of reasoning is frequently mistaken to be an effective attack upon the entire notion of nonconceptual perceptual awareness. Accordingly, Sellars concludes with a statement of "psychological nominalism"; "*(A)ll* awareness of *sorts, resemblances, facts,* etc., in short, all awareness of abstract entities—indeed, all awareness, even of particulars—is a linguistic affair."[10]

But let us retrace our steps to see what has actually happened here. Sellars has argued that perceiving something as red and round requires that one have the concepts "red" and "round." Therefore, perceiving something as red and round is not a case of nonconceptual awareness. I believe Sellars is entirely right about this. I cannot imagine what it would mean to say that x is seen as red and round except to say that x is seen conceptually. But this does not show that there is no such thing as nonconceptual awareness; it only shows that perceiving something as a certain sort of something is not an example of it.

Sellars entertains only two possible ways that I could arrive at my first perception of something as a certain sort. Either (1) the concept emerges from that something and is implanted in my mind or (2) I learn the concept as part of the framework taught me by a language community. Sellars has already attacked the plum-concept theory (1). He concludes that (2) is correct. But nowhere has Sellars entertained a case of genuine nonconceptual awareness, much less shown that there are no such cases. He just assumes from the start that all primordial states of awareness are conceptual, describes two possible sources of the concepts intrinsic to such states, rules out one source (the extraction of plum concepts) as inconsistent with the nature of concepts, and declares the other source, and with it the myth of the framework, victorious.

If we reserve the locution "perceiving x *as* x" to descriptions of conceptual perceptions, and if "*as* x" carries the conceptual freight in this locution, then nonconceptual perceptions can be described as cases where "perceiving x" is not a case of perceiving x *as* anything at all. This may seem strange to readers unaccustomed to entertaining the possibility. But I think we can see that there is nothing very strange about it. A dog fetching a ball perceives the ball, but does not perceive it *as* a ball. To perceive it *as* a ball would require the conceptual associations that dictate

---

[10]Ibid., 160.

an English speaker's use of the word "ball"—for example that it is round, frequently used in games, rolls along the ground, and so forth. The dog just sees the ball, picking it out against a background, and responds to it. The dog's optical apparatus is so much like our own that, barring strong reasons to the contrary, we should go right on saying, without discomfort, that the dog perceives—and is aware of—the ball. Sellars has not given us strong reasons to the contrary, nor has anyone else that I know of.

How can nonconceptual or preconceptual awareness be used to support "the myth of the given"? The following account of concept formation will illustrate the connection. The preconceptual child perceives the dog, the cat, the spoon, the rattle, the bright blue color, mother, and so forth. The child begins to associate one thing with another, perceiving recurrences of the same thing and of similar things. In other words, preconceptual sorting of objects and properties takes place. How does the child learn to do this? He/she is simply programmed genetically to begin to associate similar things and to have similar expectations concerning them. The existence of preconceptual sorting shows why it was important earlier to be very clear about Sellars's use of "sort." Sellars uses it only when concepts are involved, when it is a case of perceiving something *as* a certain sort of thing. Prelinguistic sorting takes place prior to concepts and explains the discriminating behavior of children in response to what they see, hear, and touch. Children recognize familiar things and properties despite lacking language to say how they do it. Prelinguistic sorting is well under way by the time the child is ready to learn the word language of its human community.

The child begins the word language at a quite primitive level by attaching "words" to individual objects. At first the language teacher capitalizes on the sorting the child has already done. The child attaches "names" to things he/she has already perceived and sorted prelinguistically. The child does this by learning how to use and interpret simple ostensive gestures. These first "words" are not yet the, English words they more or less sound like. The child is still operating in a framework far more primitive than full-blown English. A rich range of conceptual associations for "ball" is not yet in place, but the road to the associations of mature language crosses at some point the threshold from preconceptual sorting to conceptual sorting, with the latter built quite firmly on the foundation of the former. The child perceives the dog nonconceptually, watches it come and go , distinguishes it from other things.

In due course the child is taught to call it "dog." Eventually "dog" becomes part of a sufficiently rich framework that we are willing to say the child means by "dog" pretty much what we adults mean by it.

This account of concept formation in the observation framework includes four significant steps:

(1) The child is non- or preconceptually aware of things and their properties by seeing, hearing, touching, smelling, and tasting.

(2) As a result of this awareness the child begins to sort things and their properties nonconceptually according to their similarities and differences. This sorting response to perceived similarities and differences is a genetic trait without which it seems language learning would be impossible.

(3) The child is taught to attach "words" to some of the things it has sorted. To this end the child learns to use and interpret ostensive gestures.

(4) "Words" learned in the primitive, ostensive language game become incorporated into a richer framework, so that the child is finally able to use these words approximately as mature speakers do.

This account is a statement of the myth of the given because it holds (1) that the original bases for concept formation are things themselves and their properties; (2) that the awareness of things themselves and their properties results in prelinguistic sorting according to perceived similarities and differences; (3) that "words" in the primitive ostensive framework are learned by attaching them to objects and properties thus sorted; (4) these "words," their meaning and use already imbedded in things themselves, are enriched by their incorporation into the full language framework. This incorporation is guided and limited by their attachment to perceived things themselves.

It is in this way that the observation framework has been given to us. This is not to deny that much of what has been given to us up to now may not be given in the future. All the trees and dogs could die and never be seen again. Words pertaining exclusively to them and their properties would then cease to be used to make literal observation reports. Everyone might catch an eye disease and go blind so that color terms might face the same fate as the terms "dog" and "tree." But these possibilities do not undermine the givenness of the trees, dogs, and colors that we perceive today. The truth of the perceptual reports we make today will be unaffected by changes in environment or injuries to our sense organs next week or next year. The trees, dogs, and colors I see now are given now.

With this hypothesis dawns the view that observations are not merely neutral in helping decide between competing scientific theories. They are neutral in the more radical sense that Popper took for granted. Observations give us special access to things-themselves and offer a ground or foundation for knowledge. Much more needs to be said about how this foundation works, and I hope to say a great deal in the next few chapters. But before laying out the positive theory further, I shall examine Richard Rorty's attack on the myth of the given, which he tries to derive from his successful demolition of something called "correspondence theory."

Chapter III

THE MIRROR OF NATURE

Richard Rorty's *Philosophy and the Mirror of Nature* offers a definitive attack upon the correspondence theory of truth. Rorty says he borrows heavily from predecessors (principally Wittgenstein, Heidegger, Dewey, Sellars, and Quine) in drawing up his attack, but he presses it to the heart of recent analytic philosophy in a way that no one else has done, a successful tour de force.

Rorty believes his arguments also deal deathblows to the myth of the given and associated forms of foundationalism. He assumes that to demolish correspondence theory is to demolish all foundationalisms as well. As we shall see, this assumption is the great flaw of the book.

The fundamental folly of correspondence theory can be stated briefly. According to a common version of it, we have language on one side and the world on the other. To discover whether sentences in the language are true, we simply look over at the world to see if the sentences correspond with or "mirror" the way the world is. Truth rises or falls with the degree of mirroring success. The trouble is that if language is kept on one side and the world on the other, then one must do one's looking at the world nonlinguistically. But then how can such nonlinguistic lookings confirm or deny the truth of sentences? In order to see that "The cow is in the barn" is true, one must be able to see *that* the cow is in the barn. In other words, one must be able to see the cow in the barn linguistically. But then one is no longer keeping language on one side and the world on the other. Language is, and must be, on both sides of the correspondence. One can no more justify sentences by looking at the world nonlinguistically than one could, in the phenomenalist incarnation of correspondence theory, confirm the phenomenal appearances by sneaking up on the world and seeing it non-phenomenally. Rorty sees the quest for a theory of reference to be just this sort of hopeless effort to start with language on one side and the world on the other and then bring the two together.[1] He cites Putnam's recantation of "metaphysical realism" as support for his own view that this is all that theories of reference come to.[2] If Rorty and Putnam are right in their analysis, it is a devastating criticism indeed.

Rorty claims to be simply following Sellars in his attack on the myth of the given; but, in fact, he changes the argument in one important way. Rorty does not deny the existence of prelinguistic awareness, as Sellars does. Rather, he denies that it can be in any way relevant to how we justify our beliefs. And if prelinguistic awareness has nothing to do with justification, it can give no support to the myth of the given.[3] The given must, after all, be given at some point to our knowledge, if it is to serve as a foundation of knowledge—and knowledge requires justification. Why does Rorty assume that prelinguistic awareness is entirely irrelevant to justification? The answer flows from his attack upon correspondence theory. Prelinguistic awareness is nonlinguistic awareness. Nonlinguistic awareness of the world has no connection whatever with justification because, as Rorty has already shown, one cannot look at the world nonlinguistically and then look at one's beliefs to see if the two fit. Only linguistic awareness of the world will enable one to confirm or disconfirm one's beliefs. Therefore, the argument concludes, prelinguistic awareness is entirely irrelevant to justification.

As Rorty himself puts it, prelinguistic awareness cannot support the myth of the given unless there is "some connection" between prelinguistic awareness of x and knowing what sort of thing x is.[4] Rorty dismisses this connection by pointing out that prelinguistic awareness of x is at best only an "insufficient and unnec-

---

[1]Richard Rorty, *Philosophy and the Mirror of Nature* (Princeton: Princeton University Press, 1979) 293.

[2]Ibid., 294-99.

[3]Ibid., 182ff.

[4]Ibid., 184.

essary causal condition" for knowing what sort of thing x is. This last point is correct, but a red herring. That prelinguistic awareness be a necessary or sufficient condition for knowledge is not required by the myth of the given, nor does Rorty himself try to show that it is. The defender of prelinguistic awareness of x admits that, of course, it is not a sufficient condition for knowing what sort of thing x is. If it were, that would mean there is no such thing as *pre*linguistic awareness (assuming, as Rorty does, that all knowledge is linguistic). And it goes without saying that there are other ways to learn about any x than by perceiving it, and that therefore no perception of x, either linguistic or prelinguistic, is a necessary condition for knowing what sort of thing x is. But neither of these points makes any dent whatever in the myth of the given.

The issue here is whether Rorty's attack upon correspondence theory also defeats the myth of the given. The error of correspondence theory is that it sets up a problem impossible to solve and then tries to solve it. Once we start with the assumption that awareness of language and awareness of the world are completely separate domains of awarness, there is no way to get the two domains together, by rules of justification or otherwise. We have seen three ways to avoid setting up this impossible problem. The first is the way taken by Sellars, to say that *all awareness* is a linguistic affair and rule out nonlinguistic awareness of the world altogether. The second, Rorty's way, is to insist that prelinguistic awareness has absolutely nothing to do with justification; the latter takes place entirely within the linguistic domain. While Sellars denies that there are two kinds of awareness to be brought together, Rorty admits that there are two kinds of awareness, but denies that we have any need to bring them together. Since we don't need to bring them together, the impossibility of doing so will not disturb us. I have offered a third way to avoid the problem: show how language emerges from prelinguistic awareness of things and their properties—so that there never is any problem of language and the world being separate and in need of joining. Linguistic awareness emerges from prelinguistic awareness. The two sorts of awareness are joined from the moment language begins.

Rorty was right to criticize correspondence theory by denying that one can justify one's beliefs by taking nonlinguistic peeks at the world to see if language and world correspond. But he then proceeded to take the correspondence theory problem too seriously himself, assuming a great unbridgeable abyss between linguistic and prelinguistic awareness that keeps justification entirely on the linguistic side and renders the prelinguistic side irrelevant to justification. There is no such abyss. My belief that the ball is red is justified by my seeing the red ball as a red ball, that is, by seeing it linguistically. But a child learns to use such words as "red" and "ball" in the first place by seeing things that are red and seeing things that are spherical, sorting them prelinguistically according to their similarities and differences, and attaching the words of a primitive ostensive framework to them. This primitive ostensive language is finally enriched by enough further complexity to count as English, Hindi, or whatever. We can see how, in this way, prelinguistic awareness is fundamentally relevant to justification, giving us the things and properties to which our most primitive words attach. Preoccupied by the problem of correspondence theory, Rorty assumes that prelinguistic awareness cannot possibly be relevant to justification and therefore that it offers no support to the myth of the given. What I have shown is how it is relevant to justification and thereby does support the myth of the given. In my view, the dogs, cats, people, colors, and shapes we see are given to us; from the start our language is built on them, and not the other way around.

This last point should not be taken to mean that, in my view, frameworks cannot affect the way we perceive things. They surely can. A woodworker is likely to notice and understand many things about a piece of wood furniture that others would not notice or understand. Different frameworks cause us to focus our attention upon different aspects of the complex passing scene. This is the valid point made by Rorty's statements, "Intuition is never anything more or less than familiarity with a language game,"[5] and, "What we know noninferentially is a matter of what we happen to be familiar with."[6] But these statements are vague and incomplete, at least as far as perceptual intuitions are concerned. Familiarity with a language game is not enough to account for a perceptual intuition. I may be perfectly conversant with a language game using "red ball." Yet, if I look around the room right now and there is no red ball in sight, I do not have an intuition of a red ball, despite my extreme familiarity with the language game. What is required in addition to familiarity with a language game

---

[5]Ibid., 34.

[6]Ibid., 106.

is that I see a red ball. Only then do I have the intuition. Familiarity with a language game may focus my attention and increase my sensitivity, but that in itself will not deliver perceptual intuitions.

Now that we have seen why Sellars's and Rorty's attacks upon the myth of the given do not succeed, I want to suggest that these attacks were probably not the primary reason each embraced the myth of the framework in the first place. Both men wanted to put the myth to work solving other problems. Rorty, like Sellars, wanted a way to handle mind/body dualism. But his interest is also broadly political and cultural, as the presence of Dewey in his trinity of esteemed twentieth century philosophers attests.[7] Rorty believes that the myth of the given has held us captive, cramped our culture and our conversation. Desire for deliverance from these ills inspired Sellars and Rorty to construct their attacks upon the myth of the given. Arguing backwards from this desideratum would have been crowned with success, if only the attack on the myth of the given had worked. Despite its failure, however, the myth of the framework could command much sympathy if it seemed the most useful way to serve high purposes of the sort Rorty pursues. I am not unsympathetic with many of these high purposes, and much of what follows will argue that my form of the myth of the given does not stand in their way. It even adds some further ones. In this way I hope to knock out more props from under the myth of the framework.

Rorty proposes to us "the Wittgensteinian notion of language as a tool rather than mirror."[8] "Tool" is also the more promising metaphor from my point of view, but I would emphasize an aspect of it that Rorty would not. A tool, after all, is designed to fit something antecedently perceived, like words attaching to things themselves through the medium of prelinguistic awareness. The metaphor has the disadvantage that it perpetuates the erroneous impression that we can look at language and then look at the world to see if they fit. Rorty has neither of these applications in mind, however. When he calls language a "tool" he is referring to the

---

[7]Ibid., 5-7, 11-12.

[8]Ibid., 12, 295ff.

pragmatism of the myth of the framework as he construes it. I will discuss the pedigree of this marriage of pragmatism and the myth of the framework later, but first we shall try to understand better the motives that have inspired Sellars, Rorty, Quine, and others to give this marriage their blessing. The first among these motives is their desire to overcome various dualisms.

Chapter IV

OVERCOMING DUALISMS

If I think I know the nature of matter, and I think I know the nature of thought, and I think I know the criteria for reduction of thought to a property of matter, I will probably end up a mind/body dualist. If I think I know the nature of commonsense objects and qualities (such as toys and colors), and I think I know the nature of scientific microstructures, and I think I know the criteria for reduction of colored toys to bunches of microstructures, I will probably be one of three things. I will be an instrumentalist who denies that the microstructures are real, or I will be a phenomenalist who denies that the colored toys are real, or I will be both. But mind/body dualism and appearance/reality dualism also seem unsatisfactory for various reasons. And so endless philosophical battles have raged up and down the field. The myth of the framework as presented by Sellars, Rorty, and others proclaims the good news that we can at last be delivered from these (and other) fruitless philosophical bloodlettings.

Before examining this proclamation more carefully, I would like to discuss the historical roots of the philosophical problems the myth of the framework would put to rest. The sense that we understand the natures of things well enough to understand quite clearly and definitively what goes together and what does not is, I propose, the product of our intellectual love affair with mathematics. This love affair was at its most rapturous in the seventeenth and eighteenth centuries, and nowhere was it more complete than in the thinking of Galileo, Descartes, Newton, and Laplace. But it has continued unabated into the twentieth century and can be traced back to a strong beginning among the Greeks.

The present climate is most directly the heritage of the modern period, of course, but I will begin with some remarks about the classical discussions.

CLASSICAL DUALISMS

The Pythagoreans are generally credited with making the leap from explanation in terms of matter (as Thales, Anaximander, and Anaximines had done) to explanation in terms of form, that is, mathematical form. They were apparently much impressed with the discovery of the numerical ratios that underlie the beautiful harmonies of the musical scale. The measurableness of the paths of heavenly bodies led to a generalization that the cosmos was entirely an harmonious whole of underlying numerical ratios. Only denumerable ratios conferred definiteness. The absence of such ratios implied absence of structure and purpose (the latter requiring structured orientation). The structureless, the numberless was unknowable because completely indefinite. It is clear that in their doctrine of transmigration the Pythagoreans asserted the soul's separate existence, but it is not clear *why* they were convinced dualists.

Plato's *Meno* and *Phaedo*, however, take up the argument and give clear reasons for dualism. If a mathematical truth is eternal, whereas any material instance of it comes into being and goes out of being, we cannot explain our knowledge of mathematical truth by our knowledge of material instances. Socrates attempts to show that one does not really learn such eternal truths from material instances; rather, the instances are at most reminders of knowledge the soul had before it joined the body, when it contemplated such eternal truths, as it were, face to face. Both soul/body dualism and appearance/reality dualism in Plato hang upon the distinction between the eternal forms and the mutable, sensible, material instances. For Plato, as for Pythagoras, the mathematical is the paradigm case of the clear and eternal, and it is to the study of harmonics, mathematics, and astronomy that a young person's mind must turn when he begins his education (*Republic* 7). But Plato develops the Pythagorean theory of forms still further. In Socrates' discussion of the divided line in *Republic* 6, mathematical form is not the highest form; this position belongs to the pure ideas of the good, the just, and so forth. These forms are known by dialectic, whose heights can be scaled only after practice in the foothills of mathematics. Dialectical thinking is based upon absolute foundations, and the awareness of pure ideas it produces is more precise and clear because the pure ideas themselves are more true and real (*Republic* 511e).

Clarity, precision, certainty, unchangeableness characterize our grasp of mathematical truth. Plato broadens this domain of quantitative forms by adding irreducible qualitative forms and declaring these the more fundamental. But he attempts to transport these pure qualitative forms into the logical space of mathematical reasoning by giving them the clarity, precision, certainty, and unchangeableness of mathematics—and even a greater share of it. But now the premises for extreme dualism are in place. The changing world around us is less real than the forms—call the former appearance and the latter reality. That which knows the eternal and unchanging must be different from any changing body—say each of us is made up of a soul distinct from his body.

One thing for which Aristotle is famous is his blunting of the sharp dualisms of Plato. It is often not noticed that he does this by collapsing the distance between eternal, mathematical truth and the changing material world. Plato had argued (*Timaeus* 37e6-37a6) that time and therefore the material world had a beginning. Eternal truths, of course, have no beginning. The result is the maximum contrast between eternal truth and the changing world characteristic of Plato. Aristotle rejects Plato's doctrine of the beginning of time (*Physics* 251b14). For him time itself is eternal and with it the material universe. Aristotle says that the material universe and "the incommensurability of the diagonal and the side of a square" are both among the "eternal things" (*Nichomachean Ethics* 1112a22). Neither mathematical truth nor the material universe has a potency to "not be" (*Metaphysics* 1050b7-27). Even the movement of "the sun and the stars and the whole heaven" is eternal. It is not connected with potentiality for rest. For Aristotle there are eternal motions, eternal mathematical truths, and an eternal material universe. There is no need to postulate a separate, timeless domain to account for the existence of mathematical form or of any other form. Thus Aristotle sees these eternal forms abiding solely in material things, but not perishing when any particular material thing perishes, any more than the material universe perishes when any one of its constituents changes form. The eternal forms are just part of the abiding nature of the material universe. And so Aristotle denies the material world/eternal form dualism of Plato and any appearance/ reality dualism based upon it.

But Aristotle continues the mind/body dualism, or rather, he has his own version of it, very different from Plato's. He says the mind "seems to be an independent substance implanted within the soul and to be incapable of being destroyed" (*De Anima* 408b 19-20). The part of the soul that thinks and judges is eternal and therefore not perishable (*De Anima* 413b. 25-26). As we have seen, "eternal" for Aristotle does not mean "timeless." Time has no beginning and no end; the eternal is coterminous with time, that is, nonterminous. The thinking soul is eternal in just the same way that the material universe is eternal and mathematical truths are eternal. The eternal soul is the mirror image of the eternal, material world.

The center of Aristotle's discussion is found in *De Anima* 3.4. Here we are told that the thinking part of the soul must be capable of receiving the form of any object of which there can be thought. But to do this without distorting the forms it receives, it must have no form of its own. To have a form of its own would impede its reception of a new form, or at least of some new forms. If the thinking soul were warm or round, this would impede its reception of the forms cold and square (but perhaps not of the forms warm and round). Thus the thinking soul "can have no nature of its own other than that of having a certain capacity. Thus that in the soul which is called mind (by mind I mean that whereby the soul thinks and judges) is, before it thinks, not actually any real thing" (*De Anima* 3.4.). To have an inkling of what this means, we must compare this eternal soul with the eternal material world. The material world is in a state of constant change as forms rise and fall, wax and wane, in it. At no time is any of the material world "unformed"—there is no such thing as "prime matter" existing by itself. It (prime matter) exists only as a permanent theoretical substrate of changing material substances. Trees, birds, and mountains come and go; none of them are eternal. The material world of which they constitute a temporary part goes on eternally.

The situations of the material world and the mind are quite parallel. The mind is in a state of change as new forms are received and perhaps other forms slip away forgotten. At no time is any of the mind "unformed"—there is no such thing as "prime mind" existing by itself. Before it thinks, it is "not actually any real thing," no more than matter unformed is any real thing. There just is no such thing as unformed matter or unthinking mind, that is, mind without received forms. The mind exists as a permanent substrate of however swerving thoughts or received forms.

But now we see more clearly the problem with Aristotle's account. When mind is actualized by its initial reception of forms, whence does it spring into existence? In the case of matter, there is no initial reception of form, since any new form is always received by matter that already had form of some sort—a block of marble becoming a statue, for example. But mind has no form whatever and no actual existence before receiving form. It is not *something*, but how can a potency to receive form inhere in nothing at all? The account seems to break down. But where exactly lies the fundamental flaw in it?

Let's retrace some of our steps. Aristotle began by describing first the sort of receptacle the mind must be in order to receive forms. He calls this functional receptacle the "passive intellect" (*De Anima* 3.4.). He then argues for a second part of the mind (the active intellect) that is necessary to explain how the passive intellect is given the forms it receives (*De Anima* 3.5.). It is only in the section on the passive intellect that Aristotle argues that the mind is not "blended with the body." When discussing the active intellect, he assumes that this has already been shown and then argues further that the active intellect alone is imperishable.We shall focus only on the first argument; it is the hinge for the rest.

In *De Anima,* 3:4 as we have noted, Aristotle argues that the mind must be ready to receive the forms of all possible objects of thought and that therefore it cannot be blended with the body. For if it were blended with the body, it would take on the form of some part of the body. But having such "admixture" of form would interfere with the mind's receptivity to new forms. Therefore, to be open to receive all forms, the mind must not be part of the body.

Notice that this argument does not depend upon a contrast of eternal, unchanging mathematical and other forms with a changing material world that had a beginning. Aristotle has collapsed this contrast. His argument nevertheless fits the paradigm put forward at the beginning of this chapter. He claims to know the nature of "body," the nature of thought, and that the latter cannot be a property of the former. To arrive at this conclusion he makes assumptions about the nature of body and the nature of thought that seem highly questionable. Apart from these assumptions, all Aristotle seems entitled to say is that the form of the mind must be such as not to interfere with the accurate reception of new forms. Clearly, a distinction must be made (as Aristotle himself does) between having a form in such a way as to *be* something (of that form) and having a form in such a way as to know something (of that form). Why should we grant Aristotle his assumption that having form in the first way interferes with having form in the second way? Maybe it just doesn't.

Thomas Aquinas (in *Questiones De Anima,* Q 14) illustrates Aristotle's point with an example. He claims that the pupil of the eye lacks color so that it can be receptive to the forms of *all* colors. If the pupil had its own color, it would distort the received form of color and distort our perception of color. But this example precisely indicates the problem with Aristotle's (and Aquinas's) argument, seen from a twentieth century perspective. If the pupil of the eye is colorless so as to receive indifferently the forms of all colors, then it seems it should turn green when one sees green and turn blue when one sees blue. It does not (as Aquinas admits in *Summa Theologiae,* I, Q 78, A 3). What then turns green or blue when one sees green or blue? The retina has its own color and therefore does not satisfy Aristotle's requirement of color neutrality. The optic nerve and brain also have their own colors. No one thinks they literally turn green when one sees green. It seems that no part of the apparatus of sight literally turns green when one sees a green object. But then what can it mean to say that the form of green must be received by the sense of sight if one is to see a green object? It can only mean that this "received form of green" is the form of green in an "analogical," not literal, sense. To receive the form of green necessary to see something green is only to be in the sensory/neurological state that corresponds with seeing green. But if this is all that is meant by "receiving the form of green," then already being a certain color does not interfere with or distort it. The colors of the retina, optic nerve, brain, and so on are, as such, irrelevant to what goes on when one sees a green object. They do not distort the green color that one sees.

It would appear, then, that in the case of color perception, having a form so as to be something of that form (the retina having the form pink so as to be pink) does not interfere with having a form so as to perceive something of that form (a person seeing a green olive). The second way of having the form green is a matter of neurophysiology, not of turning green. So much, then, for a key premise in Aristotle's argument for bodiless operations. Aristotle had said that the intellect must have no material form whatever of its own because this would interfere with reception of the forms needed for knowledge of all material things. He concludes that the intellect must operate independent of the body. But once we properly distinguish between the two ways of "having form," illustrated by color perception, we see that the intellect might very well have its own material form without this form distorting the forms by which it knows. Operation independent of the body is therefore not required to explain how the intellect can be open to the knowledge of all of nature. The Aristotelian argument for residual dualism is completely deflected.

Aquinas wanted to avoid saying that we come to know a tree by having a little tree in our heads (or wherever). To have such little trees would be, in his view, to receive the form of the tree materially. I gladly concede that Aquinas is right to deny this is how we do it. The concept "tree" is not a little tree in the head, a particular tree image on the mind. Rather, "tree" is capable of application to trees of many shapes and sizes. This is what it means to say it is a "universal." It follows that, if we define "x materially receives the form 'tree' " as "x becomes a particular tree" or "x becomes or has a particular tree image"—then "x receives the concept 'tree' " is clearly not an instance of "x materially receives the form 'tree'." Consequently and by definition, receiving a concept is an *immaterial* reception of a form. But this is trivial, for now we have given "material" and "immaterial" such restricted meanings that they have no clear consequences for the issue of mind/body dualism. *On this definition of "immaterial,"* it seems entirely possible that bodies, say, of very great neurological complexity, could receive forms "immaterially" when they come to know. The wording is paradoxical, but only because "body" and "matter" are no longer being cut from the same cloth: a body knowing by means of "immaterial forms" is no longer a contradiction in terms. To conclude otherwise is to commit the fallacy of equivocation.[1]

But this is precisely the danger of proceeding in such an a priori manner, striking definitions prematurely. To do so is an attempt to apply a definitive deductive (mathematical) method to an issue

---

[1]It is well known that Aquinas does not hesitate to use premises drawn from Christian revelation. My criticism of him here is, in effect, a suggestion that his argument for the subsistent immateriality of the human soul depends in part on just such premises, despite appearances to the contrary. My criticism is, of course, concerned to evaluate only the *philosophical* completeness of his argument. Hence my denial that the sort of "immateriality" required for his analysis of human knowledge is *subsistent immateriality*.

that requires further empirical research. The question whether living human bodies are capable of "immaterial activities" such as having universal concepts is one that waits upon a fuller understanding of "body" than we have yet achieved, or may ever achieve. There is no metaphysical shortcut to an answer to this question. An attempt to find one will flourish, only to flounder, upon unfounded assumptions about matter, not as defined in some system, but as the actual multi-formed stuff of the universe.

There is another fundamental objection to the Aristotelian argument for a separable mind. It involves not the nature of matter, but the nature of thought. As we have seen, Aristotle assumes that the pathway to accurate knowledge requires a pure and unaffected substrate to receive the forms. The picture is of a form being imposed upon the unresisting, passive intellect. But this is the mistake we discussed earlier, the mistake of thinking that concepts such as "shoe" or "horse" can come to us as isolated singularities to be patched together later in a framework. The facts point in the opposite direction. It is generally much easier to teach a new concept to someone who already knows something about the related subject matter than to someone who does not. Lack of previous form is in such cases a disadvantage. Once we dispense with the notion that purer substrate means better learning, we can recognize the ideal of a pure potency mind as a metaphysical gaffe. Positive dispositions enhance the capacity to receive form, and these positive dispositions include the form of an appropriate framework already in place. But, if this is so, Aristotle's assumption that antecedent form must interfere with the reception of consequent form collapses. His argument for a separable mind depended on this assumption.

Enough of this jousting with the ghost of Aristotle, however. What has been said is sufficient to indicate the basis for my judgment that, after brilliantly sidestepping what had seemed to be the dualistic implications of eternal mathematical truths, the Aristotelians and Thomists failed to overcome dualism as successfully as they might have. Eventually, however, the Aristotelian advance was all but swept away by a new wave of obsession with logical/mathematical truth that inundated the academic mind of Europe in the seventeenth century. And soon all the dualisms seemed to be strutting about again, more vigorously than ever before.

MODERN DUALISMS

René Descartes is rightly regarded as the epitome of the new mathematical age. In his writing we find mind/body dualism and appearance/reality dualisms restated in extreme form. Richard Rorty notices a difference between Descartes' notion of "thought" and the notions held by Plato, Aristotle, and Aquinas. Descartes "used 'thought' to cover doubting, understanding, affirming, denying, willing, refusing, imagining, feeling," and even dreaming.[2] For the earlier philosophers, thought was connected with knowledge-by-universals and did not include any kind of imaging or sensing. The latter were regarded as qualitatively particularized and therefore activities of the body. Descartes considered all his kinds of thought to be activities of the separable soul. Rorty and Wallace Matson[3] wonder why Descartes changes the meaning of "thought" in this way. The common factor Rorty finds in Descartes' array of thoughts is "indubitability"—the fact that the subject cannot doubt that he has them. Rorty concludes that for Descartes "clear and distinct perception became the mark of the eternal, and indubitability the mark of the mental." Rorty's taxonomy seems right, but why did Descartes follow it? I think the reason Rorty's analysis gets no further than it does is that he restricts it to Descartes' "philosophical works,"[4] *The Meditations, Discourse,* and *Objections and Replies.* I believe the key to what Descartes was doing can be found only in the relationship between these works and *The Principles of Philosophy.*

The issue becomes greatly clarified if we see Descartes as primarily a defender and promoter of the mathematical/mechanistic view of the physical universe, and only secondarily as an epistemologist. On this view Descartes' primary objective was to make the world safe for Galilean science. The seventeenth-century route from fascination with math to mind/body dualism was not the Platonic route taken centuries earlier. Plato required an adequate knower of eternal mathematical truths and postulated a preexis-

---

[2]Richard Rorty, *Philosophy and the Mirror of Nature* (Princeton: Princeton University Press, 1979) 47.

[3]Ibid., n. 15.

[4]Such terminology is, of course, anachronistic. Following the usage of the day, Descartes would have regarded all his work as "philosophical," including his magnum opus of physical science, which he called *The Principles of Philosophy.*

tent, immaterial soul. The path to the separable soul was for Descartes more indirect. Descartes' primary desideratum was a physical universe that could be understood entirely in terms of mechanics. A physical universe made up entirely of the discretely measurable would be a universe entirely subject to the methods of the new science.

All that was not discretely measurable and therefore not, it was thought, subject to mathematical/mechanical laws was relegated to the "mental." The objective was not so much to save mind from science as to save science from the non-mechanical, to lift the burden of the unmeasurable off the shoulders of the physical world. And so we have, to start with, the distinction between primary and secondary qualities. The primary qualities are those that are subject to measurement: force, mass, motion, and dimension; secondary qualities such as colors, hotness, and coldness could not be handled in the same mathematical way. Consign them to the domain of the mental. The result is the one we have already rehearsed: "thought" for Descartes includes imagining, willing, and dreaming—to the amazement of Aristotle and Aquinas. Once all such qualities have been dusted into the mental bin, the new mechanics has a clear field to survey and analyze the physical universe. Thus construed, the entire nature of the material world could be known clearly and distinctly, that is, mathematically.

The nature of "thought" was far more elusive, however. No clear mathematical analysis was available here. But one thing was clear and distinct about "thoughts"—the fact that we cannot doubt that we have them. On this point they too share in mathematical truth. That it now seems to me that I am sitting in this chair is as clear to me as the simplest axiom of geometry. Thoughts remained somewhat mysterious, but awareness was certain; indubitable consciousness was seen as the nature of mind, just as the clearly and distinctly measurable was seen as the nature of body. The neatness of all this, to a passionate advocate of the new mechanics, must have been exhilarating. The neatness carries even further when we realize that a principal danger to the new science was the objections of the religious. Separating the domain of the spirit from the domain of matter kept the new mechanics from threatening religion and disturbing the religious faith of believers (whose ranks, it seems, included Descartes, Newton, Locke and Galileo).

Descartes' achievement was a strong form of appearance/reality dualism as well. Certain consciousness, including perceptual consciousness, was consciousness of ideas. In the case of perception, how can we be sure that the ideas correspond to the way things are? Indeed, the distinction between primary and secondary qualities undermines the hope for correspondence. How reliable is our access to the primary qualities? Descartes argues for their existence by invoking God, who would not fool us about the mathematically clear and distinct. Later thinkers like Berkeley, Hume, and Kant find this deus ex machina quite hopeless and turn appearance/reality dualism into skepticism. The irony of this result was overwhelming. Descartes set out to give the science of mechanics solid footing in the physical universe by excluding from that universe all but primary qualities; but by conferring so much upon the domain of the mental, he gave the mind a completeness that closed it in upon itself with no access left to any material universe over the rainbow.

This bizarre result sent out a call for Kant's attempt to save science anew. Kant's challenge was to make respectable a science that was only about appearances. He tried to do this by re-grounding all the mathematical and mechanical necessities studied by science in the a priori structures of the mind. Hegel pushed the argument the final centimeter by denying the existence of the unknowable thing-in-itself. What had started as dualism ended in monism. What had started with an effort to lift the mental off the shoulders of the physical ended with the mental swallowing the physical without a trace. The physical too became an aspect of Mind.

TWENTIETH-CENTURY VARIATIONS

It might have seemed that the desire to overcome the problems made for us by Descartes, Locke, and the others, had been satisfied. But almost immediately arose a sense of discomfort with the "metaphysical" aspects of Hegel's solution. This discomfort was especially strong in England and the United States, where the Kantian and Hegelian trains had made only brief stops anyway. Hegel, Bradley, and other idealists overcame dualism at the cost of telling us the world is very different from the way it seems. Russell and Moore revolted against such postulates as the World Spirit and the denial of all distinctness among things. Such views, they argued, fly in the face of our most evident experiences. Even Dewey found it necessary to break with idealism because it rode roughshod over the data of experience. Husserl, in a different way, rallied the Continental reaction with his cry, "*An die Sachen Selbst*"—championing a return to the things of experience.[5]

The trouble with Russell's attempt to revive realism was that it took up anew the old love affair with mathematics, this time in the form of modern logic and linguistic analysis. This led to indirect realism in perception theory. (Colors were still not *reducible* to primary qualities.) This dualism raised the old skeptical problems. Philosophies of language from Frege to the present have offered theories of reference trying to explain how the logically reconstructed language hooks onto a very different world. Appearance/reality dualism was back. And so was mind/body dualism. Assorted behaviorists and identity theorists sought imaginative ways to circumvent or reduce the obdurately mental. Finally, upon this scene of rampant *déjà vu* strode the myth of the framework, offering to do what Hegel did, but without the metaphysics. The monistic media were now to be various frameworks. Frameworks seem more familiar to us than the World Spirit and tax our credulity less. Here was Hegel in a minor key, like a few plain harmonies compared to Beethoven's Ninth Symphony.

It is time to look in more detail at the solutions the myth of the framework purports to offer. It is important to keep in mind what the myth is trying to solve. Wilfrid Sellars is concerned to show how we can resolve the conflict between the commonsense view of the world and the scientific view of the world, once we understand they cannot both be true. Part of this general conflict is the one between the commonsense mental (beliefs, images, pains, and so forth) and neurophysiology. Rorty hankers for the final defeat of correspondence theory in all its forms and consequently of the mind/body dualism that flows from it and gives it support. Both

---

[5]A list of the relevant works would include the following: Bertrand Russell's early realism is found in his *Principles of Mathematics* (Cambridge: Cambridge University Press, 1903); "Meinong's Theory of Complexes and Assumptions," *Mind* 13:3 (1904): 204-19; and "The Monistic Theory of Truth," in *Philosophical Essays* (New York: W.W. Norton, 1910).

Moore's early realism is best exemplified by "The Refutation of Idealism," in *Philosophical Studies* (New York: Harcourt, Brace, and Co., 1922).

Husserl's early realism is shown in "Philosophy as Rigorous Science," *Logos* 1:4 (1910-1911): 289-341, and also more generally in *Logical Investigations* (New York: Humanities, 1970) vol. 1. The latter was originally published in German at Halle in 1901.

Dewey's gradual shift from monistic idealism to naturalism and pluralism culminated in his *Experience and Nature* (Chicago: Open Court, 1925).

men are on the warpath against dualisms, and the appeal of the myth of the framework they promote lies largely in the sympathy many of us have for their side in these battles. The strategy of the myth of the framework is to see both sides of these conflicts as nothing more than functions of frameworks. There are no givens on either side that require our ultimate respect or that need to be preserved. Once we see things this way, we can begin to be much more relaxed about these conflicts because we can treat them as we have traditionally treated conflicts between competing scientific theories. Either we can continue to use both frameworks because they both continue to be useful; or if it seems more expedient, we can give up one framework entirely and go on living with only the other.

To help us to see our beliefs, pains, and mental images as just dispensable theoretical posits, Wilfrid Sellars invents the myth of Jones.[6] Jones is a fictional ancestor who posited various internal states of human beings to explain their behavior, especially their verbal behavior. Among these were states of consciousness involving beliefs, mental images, and pains. Once Jones had taught people this framework of internal states, they soon began to notice they were able to introspect pains, beliefs, and mental images, that is, each person was able to tell when he had various kinds of consciousness without having to infer from his own behavior. Humans have maintained this ability, the heritage of Jones's genius, to the present time. It is only recently, with the rise of new sciences and particularly of the neurosciences, that we have had the chance to give human behavior a whole other set of explanations that seem complex enough to carry the burden. There appears to be no way, however, to run a one-to-one correspondence between Jonesian "thoughts" and neurophysiological lobes, synapses, and ganglia. The thoughts are not reducible by the mathematical/logical procedures that are supposed to be relevant. But if we just remember the myth of Jones, we will be neither pained nor nervous. Our beliefs and mental images were just posits anyway. In the Sellars application of the myth of the framework, we are told that in our more rigorous philosophical moments we should think of the Jonesian posits as not real, as superseded by the synapses and ganglia with their greater explan-

[6]Wilfrid Sellars, *Science, Perception and Reality* (New York: Humanities Press, 1963) 188ff.

atory power. But we may go on using the Jonesian framework for the time being, as long as we realize we do so only for, perhaps temporary, convenience.

The myth of Jones could be regarded offhand as just a silly story, were it not for its connection with Sellars's attack upon the myth of the given. If the attack on the myth of the given had worked, the theory/given distinction would have collapsed. If it had worked, we could have invented Jonesian myths to cover absolutely any domain of discourse, no matter how well entrenched or familiar, to loosen our attachments to it and mellow out our sense that something momentous is at stake when new frameworks conflict with old ones. As we shall see, Richard Rorty has entered more deeply into the spirit of mellowness than Sellars had when he wrote "Empiricism and the Philosophy of Mind" (1956 and before). At that time Sellars talked as though he believed there were still big issues at stake; he saw himself as a champion of science against the denigrations of the instrumentalists. It is to that part of Sellars's use of the myth of the framework that we now turn.

Sellars argued that the commonsense image of the world and the scientific image of the world are in conflict because the colors of the commonsense image are not reducible to the properties of the microstructure (as, say, physics describes it). However, the myth of the framework tells us that colors aren't givens anyway. (Everybody already knew the microstructures are not givens.) Therefore, if it seems advantageous, we will just give up the commonsense image (of blue tables, green eyes, and yellow lights) for an entire absorption in the scientific image (of spinning electrons, zapping synapses, and so forth). Sellars is not content to leave us with the easygoing view that—oh well—let's not worry too much about these conflicts, they are only two frameworks, after all. Rather, he insists that in our heart of hearts we ought to believe that the commonsense framework is wrong and the scientific framework is right. He says we ought to believe this because the scientific framework has more explanatory power. But this seems to show that Sellars was still fidgety. It's as if Jones, after inventing his myth, wasn't able to introspect his own state of mind, even though his students could introspect theirs. So Sellars, one of the inventors of the myth of the framework, seems slow to realize that the myth implies that we no longer need winners and losers in mind/body, commonsense image/scientific image conflicts.

But Sellars has taken us a long way toward the deep mellow of the myth of the framework. He starts with the conflicts, mind/

body and appearance/reality (commonsense/scientific); and by steadfastly applying his myth, he shows how we can come out on the side of the materialists and of the scientific realists. This will enable us, he believes, to give science the respect its great success has earned. If this sounds like the old positivist stridencies back with a new voice, it may be sufficient to observe that the old habits die hard and new therapies work slowly, even on the therapists.

Early in his philosophical career, Richard Rorty too was using the myth of the framework to argue for the materialist side of the mind/body debate. He had not fully learned the myth of the framework's message of peace—the message that it is enough to admit that there are no neutral givens on either side of these conflicts: it is not necessary to prove that one side should be jettisoned. In *Philosophy and the Mirror of Nature,* however, Rorty catches on completely. In the style of the tradition I have been discussing, he attacks mind/body dualism by offering us a myth to consider, a myth whose moral is that we need not take sides at all.[7]

The Antipodeans, according to the myth, are like ourselves physiologically. Culturally they are no more different from Americans than, say, the Germans or the Japanese. They have their great poets, technocrats, and religious and political leaders. But they lack words for what Descartes called "thoughts"—mental images, beliefs, pains, and so on. They never talk of such things, but speak with insight and feeling about their friends, projects, politics, and the states of their own and one another's nervous systems. Instead of reporting foot pain, for example, they simply speak of contusions of the foot and the effects these produce in the nervous system. (Then they typically take two aspirins.) They have what appear to us to be shorthand ways of talking about such things; so the sentences are grammatically simple and straightforward. This difference between their vocabulary and ours does not lead to any incapacity in other areas of their lives. Their general level of fulfillment and contentment seems quite comparable to our own.

Rorty wonders what we should say about these Antipodeans, as we come to understand these things about them. Should we say that they have pains and mental images just as we do, but suffer from a deficient vocabulary? Or should we accept the Antipodean view that when *we* talk about pains and mental images, we are

---

[7]Rorty, *Philosophy and the Mirror of Nature,* 70-77.

clinging to a quaint and inefficient theory to explain our behavior? In an earlier incarnation Rorty would have argued for the Antipodean side in this dispute, using the myth of Jones to argue for "eliminative materialism." But now Rorty's use of the myth of the framework has become more sensitive. He is content to point out that there is no way to decide the issue between Antipodeans and Terrans—nothing we can say against either side will prove it wrong. Once we accept this fact, we can give up our philosophical striving on the issue and relax. Once we relax, we may be willing to admit the dispute is nothing more than a matter of how one has been trained to look at things. What more can we reasonably say?

It is important to notice that Rorty tells us the myth of Antipodea in chapter 2 of his book, but discusses the attack on the myth of the given only in chapter 4. This could give us the impression that his solution to the mind/body conflict is logically prior to, and independent of, his attack on the myth of the given. This would be a mistaken impression. Rorty's myth of Antipodea depends completely for its force upon a successful attack upon the myth of the given, despite his reversal of the order. Let me show that this is so.

Rorty's myth of Antipodea, if it had to stand on its own two feet, would be nothing more than an exercise in Cartesian fantasy. Descartes tried to make heavy philosophical points by imagining deceiving demons and that we might be dreaming even when we seem most lucid. Remember the dialogue he has with himself as he sits before the fireplace. On the one side he reasons that the things he sees around him seem most real and he has no sense of dreaminess whatsoever. On the other side he reasons that there might be a dream state where he would feel just as lucid as he then does. He finds there is no way to prove the dream hypothesis wrong. He concludes that skepticism about the world we sense around us is the position we must accept until we deliver ourselves from it.

Notice the massively strong conclusion drawn from an insipidly weak premise. We need to be skeptical about all we perceive because we *might* be dreaming or there *might* be a deceiving demon. And we say the latter only because we cannot absolutely prove the demon hypothesis or the dream hypothesis false. But now we see that Descartes has unconscionably gerrymandered the burden of proof to one side of the argument. The demon and the dream must be proven absolutely false or else! Nothing has been said in favor of the dream or the demon except that such proofs against them are not available. They are nothing but bare possibilities. Those who believe that bare possibilities can legitimately be used to arrive at massive conclusions are now to be counted among the world's few true solipsists.

Others, myself included, believe that Descartes has indeed taught us something with these arguments—he has taught us that the following slogan should be emblazoned on our minds and hearts: "Mere possibility carries no evidential weight!" If all that can be said for a thesis is that it cannot be absolutely proven wrong, we ought to ignore it until such time as there is evidence *for* it. Otherwise we shall be forced to entertain seriously such hypotheses as "The middle of the moon is made of green cheese" or "The little blue men are around only when no one is looking and they disappear without a trace." Many eight-year-olds can make up stories that are unfalsifiable, and René Descartes has been given far too much credit and attention for the ones that he made up.

What about the story that Richard Rorty made up? His Antipodeans have the same kind of nervous system we have and a comparable culture. They have no "mental vocabulary"—no words for mental images, pains, beliefs. When we talk to them about such things, they become mystified and finally conclude we are enthralled by a quaint theory. Rorty might have gone on to tell us other stories in the same vein. He might have told us about the Antipodeans' next-door neighbors, the Onkelpodeans, who have no "color vocabulary"—no words for blue, green, and so forth. They talk entirely in terms of Cartesian primary qualities, with many references to things like "bundles of k-32 particles." Rorty wants to make much of the fact that, according to his story, we could not prove to these people that they are wrong or that they are missing something. He wishes us to conclude that our own grip upon such things is just a function of the framework we use. But notice how like Descartes' argument this is.

Imagine that Descartes was not dialoguing with himself concerning demons and dreams, but had made up a story about a tribe of Antifireplaceans who insisted that a demon was deceiving them. We might tell them that we are quite convinced that the end tables and lamps are really there; but they would just recoil at our blasphemy or wonder at our theological ignorance. They might charitably try to excuse our quaint, pre-revelational beliefs. It would be quite impossible, of course, to prove them wrong. Surely we would say the same thing about this version of Descartes' problem that we said about the original. Such fantasies carry no evidential weight. Untrammeled imagination only explores the fringes of logical possibility and serves up much that is bizarre and unbelievable.

It is precisely the question whether Rorty's Antipodeans, or their Onkelpodean neighbors, could, given the same nervous system and sensory apparatus *we* have, sincerely take the position they do in Rorty's account. It solves nothing for Rorty to make up a story in which they *do* take these positions and cannot be argued out of them. We can easily make up stories about people who sincerely believe I am twenty feet tall or am wearing a beard. Yet what effect would these facile fictions have upon our convictions to the contrary? No, the only thing that keeps Rorty from being classified with eight-year-olds as a contriver of fiction is his separate argument against the myth of the given. For, if there are no givens, then pains and mental images as well as colored lamps and end tables are indeed functions of frameworks. We are aware of them because we learned a certain framework; we would be aware of other things entirely if we had learned, perchance, a different framework. Rorty's lengthy discussion of the Antipodeans is at best an anticipatory heuristic that illustrates in advance what the implications of his later argument will be. Once we have seen that his attack on the myth of the given does not succeed, however, the myth of Antipodea is also rendered ineffective. By itself it has nothing to help it stand, and it cannot stand alone.

My point has been to show that the raison d'etre for the myth of the framework is the overcoming of dualisms. It is to twentieh-century philosophy what Plotinus was to ancient philosophy and Hegel was to modern philosophy. It does not raise the anti-metaphysical hackles of those who find One Big Truth hard to swallow after we have been told to call many familiar truths into question. This would seem to give its proponents grounds to hope that there will be no impetus for further realist revivals such as were led against idealism earlier this century by Russell, Moore, and Husserl. But a new realist revival is gathering strength. The first reason for the revival is, as we have seen, that the attacks on the myth of the given were not successful. A second reason, as I shall now argue, is that the myth of the framework is not required in order to overcome mind/body and appearance/reality dualisms. Once we have understood properly the source of these dualisms, we can remedy them without sacrificing givenness.

I have already tried to show that the common underlying impetus to dualism in the history of philosophy was the introduction of mathematics into our thinking about man in the universe. In my effort to undercut dualism at its source, I do not mean to repudiate mathematics. I do mean to repudiate what seem to me overstatements of its role in human knowledge. Mathematics does not give us *the* essence or *the* nature of the material universe, as the Pythagoreans believed with religious fervor and as Descartes tried to arrange. More specifically, the laws of mechanics as adumbrated by contemporary physics do not fully explain the behavior of all forms of matter. The mysteries remain great, and we should not assume that they will be readily solved by pursuing normal research as defined by current theory. From the beginning, great problems have stalked our efforts to force the universe into the shape of available mathematics; perhaps, heirs of Galileo, Newton, and Einstein that we are, we have felt threatened by these problems.

In a recent book Morris Kline shows how untenable has become the Platonic and the seventeenth-century optimism about the mathematical nature of the universe.[8] The notion that we will get nature right just as soon as we get the mathematics right has run aground in the twentieth-century. Pure mathematics has unraveled into greater and greater chaos, even while physics advances, often dramatically. But the advance of physics has involved theoretical moves that are mathematically unjustified and even unjustifiable. Nobody knows exactly why these moves work when confronted with nature. Kline's observations deserve extensive discussion, and I will not pretend to offer such discussion here. My only point is that there is every indication that our present understanding of matter in all forms is extremely incomplete. We should not overtax that understanding by reaching the grand conclusion that no form of matter can explain what we call "mental activities."

Plato, Descartes, and even Aristotle rushed to dualism because they were inclined to absolutize what we can now clearly see was a very incomplete understanding of the material world. Because matter is somewhat understandable in terms of mechanical laws, Descartes rushed to locate all that seemed unmechani-

---

[8]Morris Kline, *Mathematics—the Loss of Certainty* (New York: Oxford University Press, 1980).

cal in the immaterial mind. Because form in matter usually resists the taking on of new forms, Aristotle concluded that the mind must be immaterial, lest its own form interfere with forms by which it knows. Because individual material things come into being and go out of being, while mathematical truths are eternal, Plato concluded that, since we know mathematical truths, our minds must be immaterial. All their arguments are based upon the assumption that we understand all forms of matter, in whatever degree of complexity or organization, quite well enough absolutely to rule out material explanations for mental activities. I believe it has largely been our early great success applying mathematics to the material world that has led to this illusion of quasi-omniscience about matter. Philosophers have perhaps suffered from the impression that things are neater in physics than they actually are, and have tried to set philosophy on the secure path of neatness. When things didn't fit together neatly by applying rules for reduction, we bifurcated the universe in grand dual categories: mind/body, appearance/reality.

In the latter case, once we laugh out of court fictional demons and megadreams as reasons for holding appearance/reality dualism, we are left with the same sorts of considerations that led to mind/body dualism. To wit, secondary qualities like colors cannot be reduced to the properties of subatomic particles. Conclusion: colored things are just appearances and the microstructures are reality. But our understanding of the microstructure is still notoriously incomplete; so why are we creating epistemological problems for ourselves as if it were not? Physics tolerates a great deal of mathematical untidiness; why can't philosophy? Why do we rush to claim we have grasped definitive essences of matter and thought? What is needed in some areas of philosophy is less philosophical striving. To this extent Richard Rorty is right. But we do not need the myth of the framework to see this point. All we need do is recognize the incompleteness of our understanding of the material world. Then we can accept our introspective states as well as the colored lamps and end tables as given, even though there is no completely tidy mathematical way to connect them with what physics and biology tell us about microstructure. Perhaps we will never have tidy connections. Perhaps we will never have a tidy way to relate wave and particle theories of light. We should simply relax and be patient. Prematurely forcing the issue creates problems that push us to ever greater extremes. Our dualisms are of our own making, and grand idealisms, materialisms, and nihilisms are the extremes to which they have pushed us.

In my view, Russell, Moore, and Husserl were right to champion the fundamental importance of perception against the idealism of their predecessors. Russell and Moore, still haunted by the mathematical/ logical problem of reduction, could not ultimately shake phenomenalism or appearance/reality dualism, however; and personal charisma could not make up for the radical instability of their philosophical views. Husserl cleverly "bracketed" the appearance/reality question as it related to epistemology because he found it had stultified philosopical thought.[9] Given the history of the question, one can sympathize with Husserl's exasperation. But many see Husserl's bracketing strategy as part of a move toward his own form of transcendental idealism. I do not intend to resolve this debate among Husserl's disciples. But I will claim that he was as much a captive of mathematics and logic as Russell was; it is therefore not surprising that he saw no way to handle the appearance/reality question as it relates to real existence, except to ignore it.

Decartes had wanted to rid the material world of recalcitrant "mental" questions so he could without inhibition apply the measure of mechanics to it. Husserl wanted to rid *die Sachen selbst* of recalcitrant "real existence" questions so he could without inhibition apply the measure of essences to them. Frege's criticism of Husserl's early study of mathematics led Husserl to distinguish in *The Logical Investigations* between empirical and a priori sciences, ranking philosophy as well as mathematics among the latter. A priori sciences required, Husserl was convinced, an "Archimedean point" as their foundation. Having bracketed the real existence of objects, Husserl found this point in the Transcendental Ego, which he radically distinguished from the empirical self. Husserl believed, much like Plato, that the necessary could not be grounded in the empirical, and so we need a more worthy ground—the Transcendental Ego. Once again the rapture of mathematical necessity leads to apodictic claims about the nature of the empirical world and its inability to sustain what seemed to be necessary truths. The early twentieth-century attempt to exonerate experience/perception had trailed back the dualisms idealism had tried to sweep away.

---

[9]Edmund Husserl, *The Idea of Phenomenology* (The Hague: Martinus Nijhoff, 1973) Lectures 2 and 3.

What I am proposing is an exoneration of perception that does *not* trail back mind/body and appearance/reality dualisms. My method has been to heighten awareness that these dualisms have depended upon a megalomanic mathematical attitude. This attitude pushed philosophers to presumption about the completeness of their knowledge (1) of matter, thought, and how they may be connected, and (2) of microstructures, secondary qualities, and how *they* may be connected. The conclusion in both cases that they *cannot* be connected leads to the two dualisms I have been repudiating. Once we are cured of our presumption in these matters, the impetus toward these dualisms is vitiated. Then we can proceed to exonerate perception by claiming that the tables, chairs, and other things we see are all given. Another prop has been knocked from under the myth of the framework—its attack on the given did not work, and now there are no dualisms around that need overcoming.

My task, however, is far from completed. Mathematics and givenness have been combined in ways that remain to be discussed. The notion that there are givens goes hand in hand historically with the notion that such givens serve as foundations for the rest of knowledge. This relation of foundation to superstructure has been typically blueprinted in highly mathematical ways. Here again a mathematical ideal has caused insoluble problems for philosophy. In the next chapter I will try to show how givenness can be freed of these problems.

Chapter V

FOUNDATIONS

"Formal foundationalism" is characterized by some or all of the following four principles:

(1) Knowledge must be founded upon certainties so strong that they defy deceiving demons and dreamings. In the phenomenal realm these certainties concern how things appear, since even deceiving demons and dreamings cannot undermine something so slight as an appearance.

(2) All knowledge is reducible by logical operations to these basic certainties.

(3) A language that expresses both the basic certainties and the knowledge reducible to them is a complete language of unified science; that is, everything that can be truthfully said can be said in that language.

(4) Anything that cannot be said in a complete language of unified science is meaningless and must be passed over in silence.

These tenets embody the mathematical ambitions of modern philosophy in full bloom. Carnap and Russell showed great energy and ingenuity trying to carry out reductions of knowledge to what they construed to be its basic elements. They did not succeed, as with admirable candor they have both admitted.[1] Witt-

---

[1]Rudolf Carnap's *Der Logische Aufbau der Welt* (Hamburg: Meiner, 1974), originally published in Berlin in 1928, was his famous effort at reduction. His repudiation of this position came in stages in the following articles: "Testability and Meaning," *Philosophy of Science* 3:4 (1936): 419-71, 4:1 (1937): 1-40; "The Methodological Character of Theoretical Concepts," in Herbert Feigl et al., eds.,

genstein too in his *Tractatus Logico-Philosophicus* laid out a complete mathematical language, but he did not use certainties as the basis of his system. In fact, it was not clear what Wittgenstein used as a basis, since he gave no examples of his "simples." Perhaps the reason is that nothing he could think of would allow the proper reductions to go through. Wittgenstein's motives are the most purely mathematical and logical of all—he published a book offering a complete language for knowledge of the world, without telling us what in the world his logical simples meant. His confidence in the rightness of his language-organizing cause made him hope that getting the logic straight would win most of the battle. This was a mistake, and he later recanted more definitively than either Russell or Carnap.[2]

My defense of givenness does not include a defense of any of the tenets of formal foundationalism. They all seem wrong to me. The first requires Cartesian certitude of the foundations of knowledge and seems mistaken for a number of reasons. The most important is one I have already emphasized. The assumption is that the certainty of "2 + 2 = 4," immune to deceiving demons, must also be at the core of perceptual knowledge; otherwise, perceptual knowledge just won't be knowledge at all. Thus we are told that all our knowledge of the world is based, not upon knowledge of trees, houses, and so on, but upon knowledge of *appearances* of trees, houses, and so on. This leads, of course, to the fruitless appearance/reality dualism discussed in the last chapter. In my view, foundational knowledge is just knowledge of the things, properties, and so forth that we perceive. Sentences describing the world, insofar as it is available to us perceptually, are the basic sentences of our world framework. This basic knowledge is quite

---

Minnesota Studies in the Philosophy of Science, vol. 1 (Minneapolis: University of Minnesota Press, 1956) 38-76; and "Beobachtungsprache und theoretische Sprache," *Dialectica* 12:3 (1958-1959): 236-48 (with English abstract).

Early statements of Russell's reductionist project include: Bertrand Russell, *Our Knowledge of the External World* (New York: W.W. Norton, 1929), published earlier in Chicago in 1914; "The Ultimate Constituents of Matter," *Monist* 25:4 (1915): 399-417; "The Relations of Sense-data to Physics," *Scientia* 4 (1914); and "The Philosophy of Logical Atomism," reprinted in R. C. Marsh, ed., *Logic and Knowledge* (London: 1956). The strong form of this early project had clearly been repudiated by the time Russell wrote *Human Knowledge* (New York: Simon and Schuster, 1948).

[2]Ludwig Wittgenstein, *Philosophical Investigations*, G. E. M. Anscombe, trans. (Oxford: Basil Blackwell, 1958) 1:46-64.

certain enough. Careful observers almost never make mistakes in reasonably straightforward cases. And the overwhelming majority of unstraightforward cases can be recognized by the careful observer and caution in judgment exercised.

Although I call ordinary observational sentences "basic" and perceptual knowledge "foundational," I deny that all knowledge is reducible to them via perspicuous logical analysis. All knowledge is related in important ways to the foundational base, but not reductively. In every case of knowledge, we can make an informal statement about the nature of the connection and how, *in every case,* the observational level is foundational for it. In the empirical sciences it is typically the desire to explain observed uniformities (or non-uniformities) that moves the scientist to construct models of underlying mechanisms. These models in turn make use of analogies that are ultimately traceable to the foundational base, sometimes directly and sometimes via explanations of yet further uniformities. These explanations in turn often ground predictions, even novel ones, that can be checked only by returning to observational tests. Poets make even more varied use of picturesque speech, drawn in diverse ways from foundations in observation and introspection. Their work enables us to imagine, understand, feel, and perceive in fresh ways. When I say that all knowledge is based upon observation (and also introspection), what I have in mind is not the picture of a logical grid. It is a more informal flow from the givens at the base, through the knowledge system and back again.

The rejection of tenets (1) and (2) undercuts (3) the ideal of a complete language of unified science and (4) the exclusion of all language outside unified science as meaningless. This last loss may seem particularly disturbing. Without question, one of the most cherished goals of modern philosophy, and indeed of all Western philosophy, has been to beat back muddleheadedness. Formal foundationalism aspired to do this in a peculiarly definitive way by nailing all knowledge to the logical grid. Without the grid to shield us, what defenses do we have against ignorance, prejudice, and confusion? Our defenses are as varied as are the connections between foundations and the rest of the knowledge structure. Consistency is a strong antidote to muddle, but even consistency must be applied skillfully. Two theories may be inconsistent with each other, but we may use them both because they are both consistent with some of our purposes, for example, successful prediction or simple computation. Being well informed generally improves one's judgment, but knowing when information gathering may or should stop requires prudence and sometimes courage to decide. Being open to the viewpoints of others would seem to be a useful part of the process of understanding, but here too one can go wrong by giving in to the pressure of fads and diluting one's own autonomy and the unique contribution of one's own vantage point.

There are, in short, no ironclad answers to the problem of judging the quality of thought. To recognize when old patterns of thought are a hindrance rather than a help to understanding often requires an extraordinary subtlety of judgment and considerable detachment. Certainly a great deal more can be said about standards for good thinking; but, no matter how much is said, there will remain an irreducible informality about such standards. The standards enable us to make many clear and accurate judgments about the quality of thought, but even the standards themselves can be used unwisely by applying, for example, standards appropriate for one type of thinking to another type of thinking. Standards for research scholarship are not the same as those for more original or creative kinds of thinking, and those who do not understand the difference are likely to apply the standards badly.

Good thinking requires more than training in some method so straightforward it can be quickly mastered by everyone of normal intelligence (as Descartes thought at first his method could).[3] What is required is more like the "wisdom" Aristotle talks about in his ethical works. Aristotle goes to absurd lengths to insist that wisdom is not a matter of following clear rules or definitions—this seems to be the main point of his tightly circular definition of "wisdom."[4] We have already said much more about the informal rules of thought than Aristotle's definition of wisdom tells us about wisdom, but he was right to separate clearly his discussion of wisdom from the sort of discussion that characterizes his logical works. I would press Aristotle's point even further. What he is content to say about practical wisdom I would say about the informal criteria of all thought, including theoretical thought. These criteria are not always clear rules; and even when they are, as in the case of strict logic, how and when they are used requires judg-

---

[3]Cf. the opening pages of his *Discourse on Method.*

[4]Aristotle defines "wise action" in terms of what wise men do. *Nicomachean Ethics* 2:6.1107a1; 6:11.1143b15.

ment of a more informal nature. We can, however, say much more to elucidate these informal criteria than simply to offer circular definitions as Aristotle did for practical wisdom. I hope my earlier examples of these criteria at work show how this can be done.

In stressing the irreducibly informal nature of many of the criteria of good thinking, I am not saying they are simply matters of convention. The criteria must be justified in terms of their connection with the givens at the foundations. The connection is not solely one of logical permutation, as formal foundationalism claimed, nor is it the same for all branches of intellectual endeavor. But one does not end justification of one's general method by observing that this is how today's scientists, literati, or researchers do it, that is, by an appeal to convention. From the viewpoint of informal foundationalism, further questions are always in order. *Why* do scientists, literati, or researchers do it this way? Ultimately, the line of questioning does not end until we have a plausible explanation of how the method exploits the special position of foundational givens as our primary access to the world, whatever creativity may have done beyond logical construction to make use of these givens.

Understanding the connections with foundational givens thus becomes essential for framing evaluations of various forms of expression and communication. Good fiction is not connected to foundational knowledge the way good history is. This causes problems for semantical theories that try to offer truth conditions for "Hamlet contemplated suicide" and "Henry VIII married Anne Boleyn" by seeking referents for the names in both. "Hamlet" does not connect to the foundations by referring to anyone real. Hamlet is a character in a play, the play is fiction, and fiction does not offer the simple one-to-one correspondence required by standard theories of reference. The point of fiction is to relate in fresh ways to the world, especially to human dreams, aspirations, fears, hopes, and so on—even though the writer does not vouch for the factuality of the situations and actions he describes that evoke these fresh understandings. The grammar of sentences about Hamlet mimics the grammar of sentences about Henry VIII, partly because fiction must to some degree be treated as true if it is to make its point; but more is needed than grammar study, even the grammar study of an ideal language, to understand how fiction differs from history. By seeing how each has its own way of elucidating the foundational givens, we learn what is most fundamental about them, and about physics and metaphysics. Straight phenomenological descriptions of these comparisons and contrasts can be most instructive.[5]

In the last chapter I discussed how Descartes' desire to make the world safe for mathematics led to appearance/reality dualism by crowding all that seemed unmathematical into the immediacy of the mental. The mental thus construed seemed closed in upon itself and cut off even from the world measured by mechanics, whose cause Descartes most wanted to champion. Formal foundationalism has its own peculiar ways of implanting appearance/reality dualism. This is illustrated in Wittgenstein's problem in the *Tractatus* of finding anything in the world to correspond to the logical simples of his ideal language. When so much emphasis is placed upon making the foundational calculations go through, the connections with the world can easily be neglected and disvalued. This results in problems about hooking the logical scheme onto the world. I have already agreed with Richard Rorty that this "hook up" project of correspondence theory is incoherent, but now I want to point out another of its bitter fruits.

In the tight logical structure of language envisioned by Wittgenstein, Russell, Carnap, and others, all terms are circumscribed by strictly logical connections with other terms. There is not much "give" in the system; it has been purposely designed to rule out moves that smack of arbitrariness. But this unites the system very tightly with the particular stage of science that is canonized in its most theoretical parts. What happens when scientific theories change? Since the meanings of all terms in the system are determined by tight formal relations, a change in scientific theory implies change of meaning throughout the system, even at the most basic level. But then how are we to explain the "hook up" between successive systems and the world? Because the rigid connections on the linguistic side of the correspondence have so little give, the connection *between* language and the world must absorb the full impact of the theory change; it must be construed as flexible enough to accommodate the change fully. It is at this point that we begin to hear talk about "alternative conceptual schemes." The gist of this talk is that there have been many ways of seeing the world, all of which hook up with it, but so loosely that very different and even contradictory schemes can be viewed as hook-

---

[5]More will be said about the creative links between givens and art in chapter 10, and between givens and physics and metaphysics in chapter 7.

ing up with the very same world. But now the world is fading fast behind the veil of conceptual schemes. It finally dissolves into something like Kant's unknowable thing-in-itself. Willard Quine and Wilfrid Sellars tell us about the unschematized stimuli that are the malleable inputs from the world, subject to litigious rephrasing by competing conceptual schemes.[6] If the connection between language and the world is so tenuous as to accommodate so many and so different schemata, then it seems likely that none of these schemata—including our present one—is true, none of them corresponds to the world. The result is the scheme/content variety of appearance/reality dualism and skepticism.

As I have pointed out repeatedly, the myth of the framework has built its career and reputation largely upon what seemed to be its unique ability to dissolve these troublesome dualisms. True to form, the myth offers an antidote for scheme/content dualism. I will discuss this antidote first and then show how informal foundationalism handles the same problem. My intention, of course, is to undermine further the motives for holding the myth of the framework, while at the same time repudiating the dualisms whose excoriation by the myth have made it (the myth) respectable.

The myth of the framework can be used to reply to scheme/content skepticism in the following way. It is absolutely impossible to present us with concrete evidence that all our beliefs are false. Any such evidence would be understood, if at all, in terms of our own belief schema. But if our belief schema is *ex hypothesi* false, any understanding we would have in terms of it would also be false. Therefore we would not be able to understand correctly the evidence or to conclude correctly from it that all our other beliefs are false. For communication to take place between frameworks,the frameworks must allow that many of the same things are true. If such common ground is not present, no one on either side could have evidence that the framework of the other side is false.

Since, therefore, we do not have and, indeed, cannot have any evidence that all our beliefs are false, we should treat the hypoth-

---

[6] "Stimuli" is Willard Quine's word in his *Word and Object* (Cambridge: MIT Press, 1960) Chapters 1-3. For Sellars it is just such rephrasing that allows the "commonsense image" to be replaced by the "scientific image." See Wilfrid Sellars, *Science, Perception, and Reality* (New York: Humanities Press, 1963) chapters 1 and 3.

esis that they are all false the same way we treat Descartes' hypothesis of the deceiving demon. Since there is no evidence for it, it is a mere logical possibility; and such possibilties carry no evidential weight. From the incoherence of the very idea of an alternative conceptual scheme, the argument can be pressed to call into question scheme/content dualism itself, since the latter seems to imply the skepticism we have just found to be untenable. It is the notion of an unschematized content that has been the source of all the mischief. If we give up this notion, we are not tempted to fulsome skepticism, and we can abandon scheme/content dualism. So far the myth of the framework.

Informal foundationalism can find some useful points in this argument by the myth. It is true that frameworks must have common ground if there is to be comparison of them or communication between them. It follows that there is common ground between successive scientific theories; otherwise the theories of Aristotle and Ptolemy would be utterly unintelligible to us, but they manifestly are not. The existence of this common ground between schemata contradicts the ideal of a rigidly formalized language whose terms all change their meanings when any part of the language is revised. The fact is that most of the connections within our frameworks are of an informal sort that allow for a high degree of flexibility *within* the framework to accommodate theory change. Most of our beliefs about the sun stayed exactly as they were when we learned that the earth revolves around it, rather than it around the earth.

These observations set the stage for the following tenets of informal foundationalism:

(1) The connections between the foundational givens and the rest of a framework are not rigidly logical. Scientific theories change and leave the foundations intact. Theory changes concerning subatomic particles, for example, do not cause the colors, shapes, and textures of the things we see around us to vary in the slightest. Scientific theories are the result of creative intellectual and imaginative activity, and there is more than enough slippage between them and the foundations to keep the latter intact even when scientific theories change.

(2) The foundational givens remain constant throughout theory change. This is what we mean when we say that the objects of commonsense perception are *given.* They are always available to form a basis of comparison and communication between frameworks.[7]

(3) Since theory change can be accommodated largely by flexibility within the framework, between theories and foundations, its force is not transferred *en masse* to the connection between language and the world. This latter transfer produced the skeptical problems of scheme/content dualism discussed above. Rather, the connection between language and the world is the very strong one described earlier. Language and world are wed from the beginning by means of preconceptual awareness of similarities and differences. This rules out, from the start, the skeptical scheme/content dualism produced by formal foundationalism. The latter can now be seen as just another example of the bad results of mathematicizing epistemology.

In the last chapter I suggested that twentieth-century philosophy can be seen as a replay of the dialectic of modern Western philosophy from the seventeenth to nineteenth centuries. The replay begins with the rejection of idealism by Russell and Moore on the grounds that it rode roughshod over the data of experience. But Russell, Moore, Wittgenstein, Carnap, and others used mathematics and logic in their formulations of realism in a way that resurrected the problematic dualisms and skepticisms of Descartes, Locke, Berkeley, and Hume. When pressed by formal foundationalism, the indirect realism of Russell and Moore changes into a neo-Kantian idealism, as the changing schemata wrench our confidence that what we believe is true of the world as it is. Finally, idealism arrives in a purer form when the myth of the framework is used to show that no evidence *can ever* be given us that all our beliefs are false, thus undermining the notion of a world so independent of our beliefs that it could make them false. Just as it is impossible to imagine Hegel without Kant and Kant without Hume, so it is impossible to imagine the myth of the framework without formal foundationalism and formal foundationalism without the linguistic empiricism of Russell and Moore. Just as Hegel attacked the notion of a world independent of thought

[7]This point receives needed development in the next chapter.

by belittling Kant's unknowable thing in itself, so the myth of the framework attacks givenness by belittling the formal foundationalist's bridge between scheme and content. In both sequences, each later link in the chain depends upon a predecessor that it attacks in order to set up its own case and make that case seem compelling. Having run around this track twice, perhaps we should reflect whether we are doing more than moving faster.

I have argued that it is our long-standing love affair with mathematics that has made such fools of us and kept us running in circles. Russell, Moore, Dewey, and Husserl were right to reject idealism because it rode roughshod over the data of experience. The myth of the framework with its attack upon givenness, has, like idealism, attempted to strip experience of any privileged position. But we must be careful this time how we re-acknowledge the full force of perception, or we shall just set the head-down race in motion once again. First we must give up our love affair with mathematics. This will be painful for us, whether we are ardent as Descartes or cool as Quine. Mathematics must become one of our friends and no longer reign over all our intellectual horizons. The point of informal foundationalism is to show how this can be done. The coming chapters will continue the effort to show the way.

Before moving on to a discussion of observation and intentionality in chapter six, I would like to end this chapter with a further discussion of scientific realism. When expounding informal foundationalism, I emphasized the flexibility that exists between scientific theories and the foundational givens, such that the former could change greatly while leaving the latter entirely intact. This may look like instrumentalism—the view that scientific theories are just calculational devices to help us organize and predict phenomena, but are not themselves true (only the observational givens being true). To the contrary, I consider myself a scientific realist. I will not argue for the position here, but I think it is important to show at least that scientific realism is consistent with informal foundationalism.

My scientific realism can be summarized in the following points:

(1) Observational givens are the avenue of truth about the world. They offer the explananda for scientific theorizing and constitute the tests by which success in theorizing is measured.

(2) The strength of a theory's claim to truth depends upon its success in meeting these tests, as well as upon the plausibility[8] of the model it puts forward and its coherence with other highly confirmed theories. Of course, if a theory's claim to truth is weak, it can be used for reasons other than its truth—if, for example, it predicts successfully within a range of phenomena or simplifies calculation. But this last point does not testify against the legitimate interest of scientists to produce theories that are true as well as instrumentally successful.

(3) The strongest claim to truth is made by a theory that is structurally plausible, is coherent with equally confirmed theories, and makes successful predictions of a sort that would not have been expected except for the theory. In such a case it is unreasonable to claim that such dramatic success was achieved by sheer chance. It is far more likely that *something* at least is fundamentally true about the theory.

It is clear from what has been said that, in my view, scientific theories only rarely make the strongest truth claims. Given the rate of theory change in the sciences, a more optimistic view does not seem credible. Some theories do achieve this stature nevertheless. The theory that the earth is round rather than flat received dramatic support by the journeys of Magellan and others. The heliocentric theory of the earth's local planetary system has also received dramatic confirmation. Our confidence in the truth of these views is not just a matter of having them consistently drummed into our heads; their connection with the observational givens is of the strongest sort. It is this which justifies our confidence in their truth.

These remarks about scientific realism pave the way for a more complete discussion of the connection between observation and theory. I have laid out the general characteristics of "informal foundationalism"; in the next chapter I wish to show how it can be used to confound the view that observations are too theory-laden to serve as neutral foundations for theories. I shall also put

---

[8]"Plausibility" will be discussed further in Chapter 8.

forward an alternative to traditional talk of "intentional objects." This alternative will serve the realist cause by showing one way the phenomenalist tendencies of the "intentional object" tradition can be avoided. Hilary Putnam's problems maintaining a realistic theory of reference conveniently introduce the chapter and the range of issues to be discussed.

Chapter VI

OBSERVATION AND INTENTIONALITY

In the last chapter we surveyed the route from formal foundationalism to scheme/content skepticism and the respective remedies for this skepticism offered by the myth of the framework and by informal foundationalism. Discussion of yet another remedy for scheme/content skepticism will help us to begin our examination of intentionality. Hilary Putnam[1] and others have tried to cure scheme/content skepticism by replacing Frege's intentional theory of reference with a causal theory of reference. According to the intentional theory of reference, expressions like "caloric fluid," "the planet Vulcan," "epicycles," and "the heavenly spheres" must refer to caloric fluid, the planet Vulcan, epicycles, and the heavenly spheres, respectively. When, with the change of scientific theory, we come to deny the existence of all these things, we must deny that these expressions referred to anything in the real world. For the formal foundationalist this creates the problem we discussed in the last chapter: because the referents of our scientific expressions have been so frequently called into question, it seems we must severely doubt that any of our expressions successfully refer. It seems we must conclude that nothing we say is likely to hook onto the world at all.

---

[1]Hilary Putnam, "The Meaning of 'Meaning' " and "The Refutation of Conventionalism," in his *Mind, Language, and Reality* (London: Cambridge University Press, 1975).

Putnam's causal theory of reference purports to solve the problem in the following way. Instead of saying that, for example, the expression "caloric fluid" refers to caloric fluid, we shall say that it refers to molecular vibration, albeit it does so in a rather inaccurate way. As Dalton has taught us, it is molecular vibrations that cause the various effects of heat. Therefore, the actual cause that led to the hypothesis of caloric fluid was molecular vibration. It is this causal relationship between the expression "caloric fluid" and molecular vibration that determines reference. Therefore we can now say that "caloric fluid" referred to molecular vibration all along, although no one before Dalton knew that it did. This causal theory of reference seems to have the great advantage of keeping our scientific language hooked onto the world even when that language is later shown to be very inadequate to the world and is eventually superseded by language vastly different in meaning. In this way the causal theory of reference was thought to strike a winning blow for realism: even the most archaic theories of science could be said to refer to the real world, however inadequately.

Unfortunately, the causal theory of reference overlooks one key point. We were told in the first place that it is the past failures of scientific theories that make us skeptical of even our most loved present theories. *Now* we are told that, on the causal theory of reference, these past theories can be construed as referring to just what our present theories refer. But to what do our present theories refer? If past scientific theories referred in only an horrendously inadequate way, why should we think our present theories do it better? This, after all, was just the problem, we were told, with the intentional theory of reference: past performance made us skeptical of present performance. But if our present theories are horrendously inadequate too, then we have little idea to what it is that either they or our past theories refer. The best we can do is make that perennial vague reference to the Peircean end of inquiry. But, of course, this move is troubled by the standard reply to Peircean ends of inquiry: that we could never know when we had arrived there and, even if we did, we could still not know for sure that our exhausted method had finally brought us home to the shores of the real.[2] No, realism cannot be served by such a

[2]Of course, Peirce himself tries to finesse this point by insisting we call whatever we end up with "reality." But this is no longer "realism" in either Putnam's or my sense.

causal theory of reference. What we see instead is just another way for linguistic philosophy to turn Kantian by producing an unknowable thing in itself. And once again the banners are waving for the myth of the framework to march through and declare the unknowable untenable and the framework king.[3]

The downfall of Putnam's realism is a microcosm of the dialectic toward the myth of the framework. Parallels with the first time around the track to idealism are instructive. In preparing the world for Hegel, Kant did much more than reduce the independently real to an unknowable thing in itself. This, after all, merely continued the skeptical strains of Descartes, Berkeley, and Hume. Kant's major contribution was to show how all that had once been explained by recourse to the nature of the independently real could now be explained by recourse to the nature of mind. It was this massively enriched notion of mind that stirred Hegel's courage to declare that all is one mind, that belief in a reality independent of mind was not only unjustified but pointless—it was not needed. Mind had grown up strapping enough to be All. Hegel's philosophy was not a repudiation of the mathematical origins of Cartesian and Kantian philosophy. It was their personification without remainder. Even progress in knowledge itself was understood entirely as an internal logical dialectic, no longer dependent upon inputs from a mind-transcending real.

What the mind became in the hands of Kant, the framework was to become in the hands of Russell, Wittgenstein, Carnap, Sellars, Quine, and Putnam (to name a few). As the notion of framework became rich through studies in logic and grammar and as the connection between all this richness and the framework-independent world continued problematic, the move to the full-blown myth of the framework was inevitable.[4] Frameworks, granted, do not inspire the same passion the World Spirit did: marching through history to the tune of the universal dialectic has a grand sonority that tinkering with our framework so we can cope better

---

[3]This is exactly what Rorty does in *Philosophy and the Mirror of Nature* (Princeton: Princeton University Press, 1979) 284-95. My own approach to the realism of reference, presented below, makes use of causality, but does so without making the referents of scientific theories into unknowable things-themselves. It is therefore not a "setup" for the myth of the framework.

[4]Putnam himself dramatically gives up the ghost of realism in his Presidential Address to the Eastern Division of the American Philosophical Association in 1977. See *Proceedings* for that year.

does not have; but the difference is more one of orchestration than of melody. The point of both is to unseat observation as the locus of special contact with a mind- or framework-independent world and then to reassure ourselves that this new self-consciousness is not catastrophe but liberation. The difference in style is, in this case, mostly a function of the *Zeitgeist.* The nineteenth century thrived on grand visions of the human enterprise, after all, whereas in the midst of late twentieth century complexities, "muddling through" is seen as no small accomplishment, and perhaps as much as we should hope for.

It is to this "unseating of observation as the locus of special contact with a framework-independent world" that I now return. The myth of the framework is, as we have begun to see, the second consummation of modern philosophy's love affair with mathematics; and it is this that required the jilting of observation. But once we have pried ourselves loose from infatuation, informal foundationalism will enable us to do what Putnam could not do: show how scientific theories *are* connected with the world, and do it without displacing intentionality.

THE OBSERVATION/THEORY DILEMMA

Informal foundationalism and the myth of the framework choose opposite horns of the following dilemma: Is observational knowledge sufficiently autonomous to serve as the common foundation for very different theories of the world or is observational knowledge so tightly integrated into any current framework that, when scientific theories change, what passes for observational knowledge can change as well, leaving no common observational foundation? My discussion of this dilemma will carry further the arguments I have already made in behalf of givenness and will set up the discussion of intentionality with which I will conclude the chapter.

The case the myth of the framework makes for the second horn can be traced, I believe, to the following four general sources:

(1) the idea of redoing or analyzing our language on the model of systems of geometry or calculus;
(2) the point (made by Wittgenstein in the *Philosophical Investigations*) that words cannot be learned one at a time by simple ostension, without the activity being part of a language game;
(3) much ado about examples of theoretical terms being used in observational contexts;

(4) much ado about duck-rabbit type line drawings.

I will discuss these four sources in turn.

(1) This is, of course, the heart of the philosophers' love affair with mathematics that I have been trying to wreck. In the last chapter I discussed formal foundationalism, the initial stage of the affair. At first logic was used by Russell and Wittgenstein[5] in an attempt to *confirm* the foundational role of observation. Observational terms were seen as the primitives of the linguistic calculus from which all meaningful language was to be constructed by means of logical operations. It was soon seen, however, that the most exemplary scientific theories could not be constructed out of these observational primitives alone. Additional primitives were needed. It was also noticed that in a logically well integrated framework, primitives, including observational primitives, are definable in terms of the rest of the framework. In fact, what we shall decide to make primitive in a logical scheme is entirely a matter of convenience. We can define ABCD as a conglomerate of A and B and C and D or we can define A or B as parts of ABCD. In the latter case, ABCD would be logically primitive. (We could call it "@" to avoid paradoxical notation.) In this way observational terms were dislodged from their privileged position in the logical scheme of things. Not only were they not the only primitive terms, they weren't necessarily primitive at all. They were so well integrated into the framework that they rose or fell with the framework as a whole—voilà, the myth of the framework.

But the last sentence does not follow from what goes before it. An example will make this clear. The planet Venus can be defined in terms of Ptolemaic epicycles as the planet that cuts a particular dipsy doodle through the cosmos. Suppose Kepler convinces us that Venus, like the earth, goes around the sun in a rather plain ellipse. Now we can redefine Venus in terms of its position in the Copernican solar system. What about Venus is given up when we switch from epicycles to solar system? Only its definition in terms of epicycles. But this was far from all we knew about Venus, nor was it the only way we could have defined it. We could have defined it as just the whitish planet that is seen at certain times in certain places, defining planet as one of those heavenly bodies—like Jupiter, Saturn, Mars, and so forth. and un-

[5]Cf. my earlier references to the reductionism of Russell, Carnap, and Wittgenstein.

like Sirius or Betelgeuse—that don't twinkle in the sky. In other words, we could have defined Venus observationally as well as in terms of epicycles. It is only the latter definition that is jettisoned when we become Copernicans; the observational definition stays intact.

It is the availability of strictly observational definitions that distinguishes observational terms from theoretical terms. The observational framework is autonomous in a way that keeps the meaning of observational terms fundamentally intact despite theory change. There *is* an asymmetry between observations and the theories devised to explain them. The theories require the explanada at the observational level as their raison d'etre. The theory of epicycles cannot be expressed without mentioning the planets whose movements the theory predicts and explains. The planets, however, do not have the same dependency on the theory of epicycles, even if no other theory has yet been proposed. The planets can be observationally defined in terms of color, location, and so forth.

The autonomy of the observational framework is not tied to logical notions of "primitiveness." In the last chapter I repudiated the notion of "primitiveness" assumed by formal foundationalism: theories cannot, in my opinion, be reduced by logical operations to observational terms. Now I am repudiating any application of the notion of "primitiveness" which assumes that a life language is a completely integrated system, either actually or ideally. The autonomy exhibited by the observational part of a life language belies this assumption. It is precisely the flexibility of the observational framework that enables it to be integrated into a particular cosmology while at the same time living an independent life of its own. Observational terms are multiply definable, and this fact confounds any attempt to analyze a living language in terms of a single mathematical system. The observational framework, never confined by logical or mathematical bonds to any theoretical system, can live promiscuously, attaching itself to a succession of theories—until and unless a truly champion theory (for example, heliocentrism) comes along.

Some have thought that the autonomy I am claiming for observation was ruled out by the requirements of the rules for language games. It is to this second source of the myth of the framework that we now turn.

(2) In his *Philosophical Investigations* Wittgenstein made it clear that every word that is learned must be learned as part of a

larger system or language game. Even words learned by ostension, by pointing and uttering a sound, require that the pointing game be understood, that the learner be able to use correctly the sound he has learned to associate with a certain thing. Otherwise we should not call what has been learned a "word" at all. The fact that a word learned by ostension can only be learned in terms of its fit into a larger language game leads to the conclusion that observation terms are as dependent upon the system as the system is upon them; and this might seem to undermine the autonomy of observation. But the important question to ask here is, What sort of system is required to make possible the learning of words by ostension? It is clear that the system required need not include a general cosmology or any of the theories, past or present, that we now call either "philosophical" or "scientific." In short, all that is needed is what I call "the observation framework." What Wittgenstein has shown us is that the autonomy of observation cannot be based upon the autonomy of ostensively learned individual words. All such words must be part of a framework. Rather, the autonomy of observation depends upon the autonomy of the observation framework.

This framework includes words for all kinds of medium-sized objects and their perceptible properties. Someone quite ignorant of current biology, chemistry, and physics can say a great deal about the cat on the mat that those learned in these disciplines understand exactly, and the learned can speak in a way that is exactly understood by the less educated. They can simply communicate in terms of the observation framework. The way in which our scientific or other theories "change the way we see the world" can be greatly overstated. I, of course, realize that all the things on my desk—the pen, the paper, the telephone, and so forth.—are made up of electrons, protons, and so forth. But, frankly, I rarely give this a thought as I go about my work. I believe it is safe to say that my thoughts about the desk, the paper, the pen during the last two hours would have been exactly as they were even if I had never heard of electrons. We do not clutter our ordinary relating to the world with constant advertence to underlying structures. For very long periods of time we simply operate within the observation framework. It is all we need for many of our purposes. It is this autonomy of the observation framework that has enabled it to remain amazingly constant through various cultural, religious, philosophical, and scientific upheavals. It is this autonomy that prevents our being severed from the world just because our theories change. The observation framework goes on. In fact, it is the observation framework's constancy and the givenness of the things we perceive that would have spared us the skepticisms we have suffered, were we not beguiled by mathematics to try to make our knowledge neater and tighter than the truth could bear.

Let's take a closer look at this notion of an observation framework. How does it connect with the theories that make up the rest of our life framework? The life framework, taken as a whole, is not a single, highly integrated cloud or field of force; it is a tiered system. On the bottom level is the observation framework. It has the autonomy I have described, but is also the source of inspiration for theories. Theories have the job of explaning why the observed world is the way it is. As the initial provider of explanada, the observation framework has more or less close ties with any theoretical explanation. During the time when a particular theory holds sway, there is frequently a strong penetration of the observation framework by that theory in some contexts. This phenomenon brings us to a discussion of the next point.

(3) Thomas Kuhn and Paul Feyerabend have emphasized historical examples where changes in theory affected observation and observation statements.[6] Do their examples call into question the autonomy I have claimed for the observation framework? I think it can be clearly shown that they do not. I shall group theory-affected changes in observation under three types:

(a) New theories can direct our observational attention in new ways. There are always infinitely more things available to perception than we could ever pay attention to. We select objects for attention based on our interests at the time.[7] Among our interests, if we are scientists, might be to test or extend application of a particular theory. And so we might start looking for another planet at the margins of our known solar system, or we might investigate the behavior of light in the vicinity of what might be a black hole, or we might start checking the fronds of a particular kind of fern. Theories affect our interests and interests direct our observational attention. What we observe once our attention has been directed, however, can be described in observation terms neutral to the di-

---

[6]Thomas Kuhn, *The Structure of Scientific Revolutions* (Chicago: University of Chicago Press, 1970); Paul Feyerabend, "How to Be a Good Empiricist," in Harold Morick, ed., *Challenges to Empiricism* (Belmont CA: Wadsworth, 1972).

[7]For an article-length treatment of the "selectivity of perception," see my "Selective Perception," *Reason Papers* (1981).

recting theory. This shows that the autonomy of the observation framework remains intact. The fronds have turned blue-green, or there is a bright spot next to Pollux, or the numbers from the computer are such and such.[8]

(b) Theoretical terms can be substituted for observational terms. In this observational use theoretical terms change, of course, when theories change. Suppose a student is taught to describe the movement of heat along a steel rod being flamed at one end by saying, as he progressively touches the rod, "The caloric fluid is surging toward the other end." Suppose he can do this without mentally running through the inferences from "hot-to-the-touch" to "caloric fluid." The statement is in this sense non-inferential and in this sense observational. Suppose the student meets Dalton and is persuaded that the caloric theory of heat is wrong and the molecular vibration theory is right. Under the same observational conditions, he now describes what is happening with the steel rod differently: "The molecular vibrations are being rapidly transmitted to the other end." The theory change has caused a change in the observation statement. Doesn't this call into question the autonomy of the observation framework?

To see that it does not requires only a small amount of subtlety. To describe what one perceives in touching the rod as "the surge of caloric fluid" or "the transmission of molecular vibration" is to use figures of speech. In ordinary language we use figures of speech all the time; in rigorously worked out logical and mathematical systems we do not—in such systems the rules require univocal usage. But literal-mindedness applied to synedoche or metaphor yields absurdity. Those who model the life framework on such formal systems are likely to bungle figures of speech badly, if they fail to rule them out completely. Formalists will want a single answer to the question, Can "caloric fluid" be used as an observation term? They will then set up some criterion to decide the question, Can "caloric fluid" be used non-inferentially (as defined above) to describe what one perceives? The answer is yes. Therefore, the argument continues, it is an observation term in this usage. But, since it is jettisoned as an obser-

---

[8]This ability of new theories to direct our observational attention in new ways is important for the kind of scientific realism I espoused earlier. I said then, agreeing with Karl Popper, that confirmation of novel predictions, otherwise unexpected, is a key part of the strongest truth claim a scientific theory can make.

vation term when theories change, it follows that the observation framework is not autonomous. Or so the argument goes.

Are metaphors observation terms when used in observation contexts? Suppose the half-moon reminds me of my mother's silver fruit bowl—so much so that frequently when I see a bright half-moon, I declare, non-inferentially, "Mother's bowl is out tonight." Is "mother's bowl" being used as an observation term here? If we know about metaphors, we feel the need for a small amount of subtlety in answering. We say something like: "Well, no, it's not mother's bowl I see up in the sky, it's the half moon; but when I was a child I always thought it looked like mother's silver bowl, and so that's still what call it, especially when I'm feeling a little nostalgic."

"Caloric fluid" and "molecular vibration," when used observationally, are not, strictly speaking, metaphors; but they are figures of speech. When a word denoting one kind of object is replaced by one literally denoting another kind of object in order to draw attention to the resemblance between them, we have a metaphor. When we substitute "caloric fluid" for "heat," the substitution is not based upon sensible resemblance, it is rather the substitution of explanans for explanandum. Let's call this an "explaphor." If the student were asked, in the case given above, whether he was using "caloric fluid" as an observation term when he touched and described the steel rod, he should answer, with a small amount of subtlety, "Well, no, it's not caloric fluid that I feel in the rod, it's just the heat that everyone feels; but I have learned that heat is caused by the influx of caloric fluid, and so I call it caloric fluid, especially when I'm feeling scientific." Now, it is true that according to the theory, caloric fluid is literally there in the rod, whereas mother's bowl is not literally there in the sky. But the point is that neither the caloric fluid nor the bowl is literally perceived. The heat of the rod feels the same whether one says it is molecular vibration or caloric fluid—it does not seem to shake in the first case or feel wet in the second. The constant way the rod feels can be described in the autonomous observation framework: "It feels hot." The rest is explaphor.

We can use explaphors to explain the way theories penetrate the observation framework, but without affecting its autonomy. In some contexts it is useful to substitute theoretical terms into the observation framework. Why bother to say things like: "I see a squiggle and it is caused by a positron, according to the theory"? Just say, "I see a positron." In other words, just use the explaphor.

The context makes the rest clear anyway. If the theory changes, all the observational explaphors of the old theory get pulled; but the squiggles, the dots, and the bright blue spots remain the same. The words we use for such things in the autonomous observational framework stay relatively constant, despite revolutionary change between generations of explaphors, functions that they are of changing theories.

The attempt to define observation statements as non-inferential statements made in observational contexts is not a surprising move, coming, as it does, from those pursuing the ideal of a highly integrated logical system. Such logical systems distinguish between inferences made within the system and non-inferential system-entry intuitions. From that point of view, the special role of observation in the life language is defined in terms of non-inferential language-entry intuitions.[9] What I have argued is that a further distinction must be made: between observation terms that are explaphors, and therefore functions of theories, and observation terms that are part of the autonomous observation framework. It was the failure to make this distinction that led Wilfrid Sellars to surmise that scientific theory could completely take over the observation framework. Once we recognize that theoretical terms substituted into the observation framework are being used as figures of speech, we will be far less inclined than Sellars was to treat the autonomous observation framework as expendable. But this is, of course, just one point in my general attack on the myth of the framework, which Sellars holds, and the love affair with mathematics, which Sellars enjoys. It is not a small point, however. The concept of an "explaphor" is key to understanding how theoretical terms can both penetrate the observation framework and leave it autonomous. The autonomy of the observation framework is in turn key to understanding what I mean by saying the life language is a tiered system with the autonomous observation framework at the foundation. And the tiered system is key to understanding how realism at the observation level inspires and validates theories but is nevertheless unthreatened by theory change.

(c) A third way that theory change could bring about change in observation statements concerns the technologies made pos-

[9] Cf. Wilfrid Sellars, *Science, Perception, and Reality* (New York: Humanities Press, 1963) 328-29 and my discussion of him on this point, "The Problem of the Two Images," in William Pitt, ed., *The Philosophy of Wilfrid Sellars: Queries and Extensions* (Boston: D. Reidel, 1978) 73-103.

sible by theories. Our theories have enabled us to build such things as X-ray machines, cloud chambers, and nuclear reactors. The names we give the components of such technologies often use theoretical terms to emphasize the connection between the technology and relevant theory. If the theories that inspired these technologies and explain how they work were to change, the corresponding names for these components would probably change as well. Suppose the ray and particle theories of light were finally synthesized or superseded by a single theory. And suppose we called the central operatives of this new theory "quays" instead of "rays." We might reasonably decide to rename the X-ray machine "the X-quay machine." This renaming is no big deal. What we have said about explaphors makes it clear that this does not threaten the autonomy of the observation framework. The machine looks just the same as before and so do the X-ray and X-quay photographs it takes. Such technologies show, in a sense, the deepest penetration of theory into the observation framework: they actually change the face of the observed world. In this case the penetration comes, not merely by affecting our frameworks, but by giving us entirely new things to perceive. But seeing X-ray machines or nuclear reactors for the first time does not threaten the autonomy of the observation framework any more than does seeing gnus or pandas for the first time. The autonomous observation framework can expand indefinitely to accommodate new things perceived. Explaphors should be substituted when it seems convenient; and new technologies will, of course, be given names that associate them with relevant theory. These names and explaphors may be changed if the relevant theories change, but the autonomous observation framework will be unaffected.

(d) Ludwig Wittgenstein, Norwood Hanson,[10] and others have been interested to discuss how it is that a duck-rabbit line drawing can be seen either as a duck or as a rabbit. It is clear that the drawing itself stays the same whether I see it as a duck or as a rabbit. Therefore, it is not the drawing that changes, but I myself who change when I see the drawing first as a duck, then as a rabbit. Does this call into question the autonomy of the observation framework?

---

[10]Ludwig Wittgenstein, *Philosophical Investigations*, trans. G. E. M. Anscombe (Oxford: Basil Blackwell, 1958) 2:xi; Norwood Russell Hanson, *Patterns of Discovery* (London: Cambridge University Press, 1973) Chapter 1.

The first thing to keep in mind here is that we are talking about line drawings. No one suggests that we would have similar problems distinguishing real ducks from real rabbits. The duck-rabbit exploits the fact that a line drawing of rabbit ears can be made to look just like a line drawing of an open duck bill. To begin with, then, it would seem an inept generalization to argue from the way we handle ambiguous line drawings to problems about observation in general. Since the serious activities of science, philosophy religion, and poetry have very little to do with the observation of line drawings, it seems what we are discussing here may be a curiosity rather than a main line problem. But let's discuss it anyway.

Why does the duck-rabbit seem to create a problem for the objectivity of observation or the autonomy of the observation framework? Why should it puzzle us that a cartoon can be made to look as much like a rabbit as like a duck? Perhaps because we know that a duck cannot at the same time be a rabbit, we inattentively conclude that a drawing of a duck cannot at the same time be a drawing of a rabbit. But drawings are not like the real thing in this respect. The duck-rabbit is at one and the same time a drawing of a duck and a drawing of a rabbit. There is no ontological problem lurking among the lines of the duck-rabbit. Is there an epistemological problem? I don't see what it is. Each thing we see in this world is so manifold in its properties that we can never advert to all of them at the same time. Some properties we notice almost all the time, others frequently, still others almost never. A live duck or a live rabbit may be thought of as cuddly companions or as tonight's dinner. Neither of these viewpoints is false. Ducks and rabbits both have properties that justify either way of seeing them. Both ways of seeing are as objective as you like: Objectivity is entirely compatible with selectivity of focus.[11]

If there is no epistemological problem *here,* there is none in the case of the duck-rabbit. The duck-rabbit looks like a duck (in the cartoon sense of "looks like"), and it looks like a rabbit. To see it alternately as a duck and as a rabbit is to see it accurately and more completely than to see it only one way. Alternating ways of seeing it seems perfectly suited to the sort of object it is. It is true that when I go from seeing it as a duck to seeing it as a rabbit, it is I that change, not the drawing. But this change in me simply en-

[11]Cf. my "Selective Perception."

ables me to advert to something further that is true of the drawing—namely, that it looks like a rabbit, and not only like a duck. This capacity of ours to change focus is something we count on to enable us to perceive more of what passes before us and to make more complete use of it.[12] Even if we take duck-rabbit drawings very seriously, they pose no threat to the objectivity or autonomy of the observation framework. They just illustrate how the framework can be alternately brought to bear upon the manifold aspects of the world we perceive.

I have examined the sources of the myth of the framework's arguments for the second horn of the dilemma about the connection between observation and theory, the dilemma with which we began this section; and I have defended the autonomy of the observation framework at every point. Now I will use the liberated observation framework I have defended to address the problem Putnam unsuccessfully tried to solve with the causal theory of reference: how are we to understand the connection between our theories, especially outmoded ones, and the world? Putnam believed, remember, that realism could not be defended by using an intentional theory of reference; for, once we deny the existence of, say, caloric fluid, there would be nothing for "caloric fluid" to intend. But then there would be nothing to which, on the intentional theory of reference, it would refer. This finally seemed to undercut reference of all theories, to undercut realism itself.

But now we can use the autonomous observation framework to establish stable reference points for our theories. "Heat" is definable in the observation framework. Thus defined, its meaning did not change when "molecular vibration" replaced "caloric fluid" as its theoretical explanation. Both "caloric fluid" and "molecular vibration" refer to the underlying causal mechanism of the perceived quality we call "heat." We now know that "caloric fluid" referred to this mechanism mistakenly, but it was nevertheless this mechanism that it attempted to describe. Its connection with the world is through the quality heat that, as understood in the autonomous observation framework, stays constant through the theory change to "molecular vibration." Does "caloric fluid" refer to anything? If by that question we mean, Does caloric fluid exist?—the answer is, of course, no. But if by that question we mean, Was there something specific that "caloric fluid" tried to get at?—the answer is yes, the underlying cause of

---

[12] Ibid.

heat. We can specify this reference point by using terms in the observation framework to anchor it. In this case we tie "caloric fluid" to "heat." It seems we could not reasonably want to be more realistic about the ties between an outmoded theory and the world.

The foundational cognitive connection between ourselves and the world is an intentional one after all, and its medium is the autonomous observation framework. I have spent a great deal of time in this and preceding chapters defending observation against the many skepticisms that have been arrayed against it. Now that things seem quieter on that front, we have respite to give some attention to intentionality itself. This will complete my discussion of the realism of the observation framework.

INTENTIONALITY

In his *Psychologie vom empirischen Standpunkt* (1874), Franz Brentano says, "Every mental phenomenon is characterized by what scholastics of the late Middle Ages called the intentional (and also mental) inexistence of an object, and what we would call . . . the reference to a content, a direction upon an object (by which we are not to understand a reality . . .) or an immanent objectivity." He soon goes on to say, "This intentional inexistence is exclusively characteristic of mental phenomena."[13] These statements introduce two theses concerning intentionality: (1) all mental phenomena have intentional objects immanent to them; (2) *only mental* phenomena have intentional objects, that is, intentionality is a mark of the mental.

I shall not discuss (2) at length, but it should be noted that it does seem to conflict with at least two other standard ways of marking the mental. If we mark the mental with universality (acts of intellect) or freedom (acts of will) in the classical fashion, then mental images are not included among mental phenomena. Since mental images are intentional, it follows that some intentional objects would not be mental. On the other hand, if we mark the mental as the unextended and non-mechanical in Cartesian fashion, then pain is among the mental phenomena. Yet pain does not seem to be an intentional object. It does not seem necessary for any of my purposes to try to untangle these issues; the focus of what follows will be the ontological issues raised in (1).

---

[13]Franz Brentano, *Psychology from an Empirical Standpoint* (New York: Humanities Press, 1973) vol. 1, bk. 2, chap. 1.

By the time of the second edition of the *Psychologie* (1911), Brentano is concerned to deny that the intentional object is some sort of copy of the real object. He insists that his main point is that one can think of something even if it does not exist. The status of "intentional objects" continued, however, to be the subject of much discussion. Both Brentano and at least the early Husserl meant to use "intentionality" in the service of realism, to explain how subjects are related to objects that—contra Hegel—exist independently of the mind that knows them, loves them, and so on. Despite these, from the realist point of view, good intentions, "intentional objects" talk created problems for realism. Brentano was not the only writer with realist pretensions to use it.

Both Husserl and Meinong appear to support Brentano's view that all mental phenomena have objects, but they state the point in terms of the philosophy of language. For Husserl, the meaningfulness of an expression entails reference (*Beziehung*) to an object, regardless of whether that object exists or is "fictive." For him reference to an object and presentation of an object are the same thing.[14] Meinong distinguishes between reference and presentation: "A word always 'refers to' the object of the presentation that it 'expresses' and, conversely, expresses the presentation of the object that it refers to."[15] For my purposes, the important assumption made by all three writers—at least for parts of their careers—is that mental phenomena, or meaningful words and expressions, invariably have objects. It is a very useful feature of the realism I am proposing that it accepts objectless mental states and objectless meaningful expressions, where "objectless" excludes intentional as well as real objects.

Eventually, both Brentano and Husserl arrived clearly at this same view. Why had they made the "intentional object" mistake in the first place? Perhaps they thought that, in order to guard the realism of their theory of meaning, they had to define "meaning" in terms of reference to an object. This required objects for all meaningful expressions, even those without real objects. The alternative would have been to define meaning as a relationship among ideas or concepts. In the early years of the struggle against

---

[14]Edmund Husserl, "Expressions and Meaning," in his *Logical Investigations* (New York: Humanities Press, 1970) 2:51. This work was originally published in German as a series from 1913-1921.

[15]Alexius Meinong, *On Assumptions* (Berkeley: University of California Press, 1983) 20. This is a translation of the revised German edition of 1910.

Hegelian idealism, this might have seemed too great a concession. In what follows, I shall discuss intentionality using a Wittgensteinian notion of meaning and show how the latter can be incorporated into a realist epistemology. To this extent, my view makes peace with "idealism." I began this task earlier when I talked about the "observation framework" that provides the foundations for knowledge.

The meaning of an expression and the object of an expression are distinct. For purposes of the following discussion, I will require nothing stronger than a contextual definition of "meaning": one understands the meaning of an expression, if and only if one understands its place in a language game. This definition is compatible with there being other necessary conditions for meaningfulness, but it will provide, as it stands, an adequate basis for distinction between meaning and object. Understanding an expression's place in a language game implies the ability to connect it properly with other words and expressions and to apply it properly to objects in observation, if such application is part of its use in the language. To understand the meaning of "horse" requires that one be able to converse about horses and to recognize them observationally when the opportunity arises. The object of an expression is that to which it refers, that which it is about. "Jason's chestnut filly" refers to a particular animal that is its object. Application to an object is often *part* of an expression's use in the language; but even in such cases, application to an object is different from the object itself and does not cloud the distinction between meaning and object.

According to the realism I am proposing, the primal occurrence of "objectivity" is in prelinguistic perceptual awareness. I discussed earlier how awareness has its beginning as prelinguistic, preconceptual awareness of objects, and how language has its beginning in an observation language game in which words are attached to these objects of awareness, while at the same time being related to one another. On this view, reference is not a "problem" to be solved at some later point in the philosophy of language; it is an intrinsic part of language learning from the start. Participation in the primary objectivity of "objects of awareness" is conferred upon expressions in the observation framework via the ostensive component of language learning at this basic level. The application-of-an-expression-to-an-object that we call "reference" is learned, in the first place, by applying expressions to objects of awareness.

Now let's see how these distinctions (among "object," "meaning," "intention," and "reference") function, in a series of examples. In what follows, what I say about objects of judgments applies as well to objects of statements, and vice versa.

(1) The judgment is true, and its object perceptually present. This is of course, the most straightforward case possible. When I declare, "The cat is on the mat," because I can see the cat on the mat, the object of my statement or judgment is just the cat on the mat that I see. No additional object is needed.

(2) The judgment is true, but the object is not perceptually present. Suppose while in Washington, I say, "Dad is in Pittsburgh." Despite the element of absence—my inability at the moment to perceive Dad in Pittsburgh—the object of the judgment is still Dad in Pittsburgh. Perhaps, as I make the statement that Dad is in Pittsburgh, I have a mental image of him, standing in front of Three Rivers Stadium. Does this mental image become the object of the statement "Dad is in Pittsburgh?" Of course not. The statement is not about my mental image, it is about Dad in Pittsburgh. The mental image is a perhaps enlivening accompaniment of the judgment; it is not its object. In (6) I will discuss the status of mental images when judgments are made about them. But in the present case, the judgment is not at all about a mental image, whether one accompanies the judgment or not.

(3) The judgment is false, but the objects exist. Suppose I say, "Harry is in the basement," when, in fact, Harry is outside. The judgment is false. It therefore lacks the complete object exemplified in (1) and (2). But it has what I call a "partial object." The statement "Harry is in the basement" is about Harry and about the basement. Both Harry and the basement exist. Therefore, the statement is not completely objectless. Even though false, it refers in some way to Harry and to the basement. Suppose, when I utter the statement, I have a mental image of Harry in the basement. Is this image the object of my judgment? Of course not. I was not talking about my mental image, I was talking about Harry and the basement, even though my judgment about them was false.

(4) The judgment is false, and the stated objects do not exist, but the judgment is a case of mistaken identity. Suppose I say, "Sally's cat was on the roof of her brother's house." Suppose Sally, in fact, has no cat and no brother. Now, suppose I had seen someone who I thought was Sally's brother and had seen his house and had seen a cat that I thought was Sally's. In some sense, then, my statement was directed at these individuals. I was trying to talk

about them, even though I misidentified them. In this case too, it seems to me, we can say the judgment had a partial object, despite the mistaken identity. It now becomes clear that my notion of "partial object" can be applied in many kinds of false judgments, whenever objects for the judgment exist, even if they are misidentified. Once again, no mental images I may have had while making the judgment qualify as objects of the judgment, even though they may help me figure out later to whom and to what I was actually trying to refer.

(5) The judgment is false, the objects do not exist, and the judgment is not a case of mistaken identity. Suppose someone tells me about an invasion in order to test my gullibility. Suppose I believe him and tell others, "The Palducian army has landed." But there are no Palducians, and therefore no Palducian army has in fact landed. No army has landed. The statement to the contrary is false. It is difficult to see how we could find even a partial object for it. It refers to nothing at all. The early Brentano wanted to say that objects that do not exist can still be referred to. They were not, according to him, real objects, but intentional objects. But what problem does this move help to solve? If one ties meaningfulness to reference to an object, then one needs an object of some kind to make "The Palducian army has landed" meaningful. But if one equates meaning with use in a language game, as I have been doing, then the postulation of intentional objects is not necessary. The sentence is meaningful because of its fit with the language we use when talking about amphibious invasions (and so on). When meaning no longer requires objects, we no longer need objects for judgments or statements.

This has advantages. We no longer have to puzzle ourselves with trying to explain what sort of an entity an intentional object is—a mental image?—a concept?—an eternally existing state of affairs?[16] Nor do we have to explain how it is that people can actually be referring to intentional objects when they intend to refer to real objects and when the language they use implies a claim about real objects. It seems just as ridiculous to say to me, "You thought you were referring to a real army, when in fact you were referring to an intentional army" as to say, "You thought you were talking about an army; actually you were talking about your men-

---

[16]I discuss Roderick Chisholm's use of just such eternal states of affairs in my "Roderick Chisholm: Self and Others," *Review of Metaphysics* 33:1 (September 1979): 135-66.

tal image of an army." But surely I would have known if *that* was what I was talking about. Finally, we can avoid quandaries about whether we must have intentional objects for judgments even when we have real objects for them (as in (1)-(4) above). Having two objects, one intentional and one real, seems redundant. But to deny there are intentional objects in such cases requires us to explain their sudden appearance only when no real objects exist. Neither horn seems attractive. Better to say some judgments are objectless, but meaningful, and therefore false.[17]

(6) The judgment is about mental images. The most important thing to realize about mental images is that, literally speaking, there are no such things. The expression "mental image" is a metaphor. The primary and literal meaning of "image" had to do with statues, paintings, reliefs, imprints on coins, and, later, photographs and movies. We can mistakenly think of a mental image as something like these, as if there were a sort of movie screen in our brain with our mind's eye looking at it. It is important to deny this picture explicitly. There is no such screen and no such eye, and that is why I say "mental image" is a metaphor.

But then, what is it that is literally going on when we use this metaphor? Well, first we must acknowledge that having a mental image is something like perceiving the real thing. This is true of literal images as well and is the basis for the metaphor. Seeing a photograph of George is something like seeing George. Just how is having a mental image like perceiving the real thing? When I see George, my nervous system is operating in a particular way. When I see Harry, my nervous system is operating in a different way, and this difference is correlative to the visible difference between George and Harry. My seeing these differences in these two people depends upon differences in my neurological operations. Now, what happens when I have a mental image of George? My nervous system is operating in a way that is significantly like the way it operates when I *see* George. Similarly, when I have a mental image of Harry, my nervous system acts somewhat as it does when I *see* Harry. As a result of this similar nervous activity, I have an

[17]The claim that all judgments must have intentional objects sounds ominously like the "indirect realism" of Locke, Russell, and Moore. It sets the stage for a radical skepticism that attempts to solve the redundancy of objects by questioning the grounds or need for *real* objects. This tiresome gambit is avoided by allowing for objectless judgments. This eliminates any need for intentional objects and prevents the ineluctable thrust toward idealism.

experience that is significantly similar to seeing George or Harry. Yet this experience is very different from real seeing, not only because George and Harry are not present, but because of the evanescent quality of the experience itself. Mental images tend to come and go in a way that Harry and George could not. When we try to check memory images for fine details (How many buttons on the coat? How many steps on the stairway?), we find that our questions are usually not answered—as they would be if we were looking at the coat or at the stairway. This is why I say my brain state during a mental image of George is significantly like it is when I see George, but it is very far from being exactly like it. Precise phenomenological analysis could detail the distinction further. We do not yet have the knowledge of neurophysiology necessary to lay out exact physiological correlations.

Enough has been said, however, to prepare the way for my central claim about mental images: when I am in a state of awareness that we metaphorically call "having a mental image," there is literally no object of that awareness at all. There *seems* to me to be an object because I am in a state significantly like the state I am in when I *see* something. The similarity of the experience explains why we use this metaphor "mental image," but there literally are no such images. If there are no such images, then there are no *objects* for the state of awareness we call "having a mental image." The experience *seems* to be an awareness of an object, which explains why we use the "image" metaphors we do to describe it.

The point I have been making is summarized grammatically in the "adverbial theory" of sensing.[18] According to this theory, the way to describe my having a mental image of George is to say, "I am aware in the George manner," or "I am aware George-ly." The adverbial construction avoids grammatical metaphors that seem to give such states of awareness objects, when they have none. The adverbial theory also expresses the significant similarity between having images and perceiving. It does this by using the same adverbial construction in describing both. When I am seeing George,

---

[18]Put forward in Roderick Chisholm, *Theory of Knowledge* (Englewood Cliffs NJ: Prentice-Hall, 1966) 95-96. Chisholm puts adverbial sensings to work in setting up his own unique kind of formal foundationalism—a use to which I, of course, would not put them. A use of them more like my own can be found in James Cornman, *Materialism and Sensations* (New Haven: Yale University Press, 1971).

I can say, "I am aware of George *George-ly.*" In my view, "George-ly" indicates the neurological ground of the awareness—in this case the awareness of an object, George. When I am having a mental image of George, I can say, "I am aware George-ly," with no mention of an object. "George-ly" used in both descriptions indicates the similarity between the two that grounds the "image" metaphors of ordinary usage.

By taking this objectless tack in analyzing mental images, I do not mean to denigrate in any way their importance in our cognitive processes. Sometimes our way of thinking about objects can be very image-centered. Mental images frequently facilitate or correct even the referring activity of thought. Perhaps George has fond memories of a very warm and happy twelfth birthday when he was a child. Mental images are indispensable for recalling the happenings and feelings of that occasion. Suppose he has a mental image of Aunt Tilly carrying in the birthday cake while everyone sings. Then it occurs to him that Aunt Tilly had died by the time of his twelfth birthday. Taking further thought, he concludes that it was his eleventh birthday that he was remembering. His mental image of Aunt Tilly helped him, in this case, to get the reference straight. Only if we inappropriately generalize the standards of logic, which place a premium upon univocal language, will we think that "metaphor" is a name for second-rate thought and expression. Good metaphor makes a point that cannot be made as well any other way.

Understanding "mental image" as a metaphor accomplishes two things for the realist. It reduces still further the temptation to solipsism. The sorts of objects that suggest solipsism—intentional objects, mental images—literally do not exist. Secondly, it emphasizes the priority of perceptual experiences to imaging experiences. Objects of perception precede mental images chronologically and as an order of being. This coheres exactly with realist views about language learning and about the observation framework discussed earlier in this chapter.

(7) The judgment is about fictional objects. Sherlock Holmes cannot be said to exist in the same way that Winston Churchill existed. But nor is "Sherlock Holmes" the name of a mental image. When we hear or read stories, we are casting our attention outward in hearing and seeing, rather than inward, as in the case of mental images. To understand what sort of object Sherlock Holmes is, we must first understand that Sherlock Holmes is the central figure in a series of stories. Except for these stories, Sherlock

Holmes has no existence whatsoever. Since Sherlock Holmes exists only as a constituent part of fictional stories, we will understand what sort of object Sherlock is when we understand what sort of object a fictional story is. Such stories, like many other products of art, are images of some sort, but not mental images. A real image is as much an object of perception as any other thing we see or hear, but the way we speak about such images can cause confusion. Once again it is important to notice that we use parallel grammar in unparallel cases. We can truthfully utter sentences of the form "Sherlock Holmes did such and such" and "Winston Churchill did such and such." The grammar is the same, and we can be misled by it. The sentence about Holmes is true if it fits one of his stories. The sentence about Churchill is true if it fits the historical facts. Being true of an image (in this case a fictional story) is different from being true of "real life." The parallel structure does not express this distinction; a wider context is needed. Unless we keep in mind this wider context of the "fictional story image," we may make mistakes when we hear that "Sherlock Holmes" has an object to which it refers. We may conclude that, since there is no real person to serve as that object, it must be some sort of intentional object. But no such intentional object is needed in this case or in any other. The object is the Sherlock Holmes of the stories, and the stories are real (not mental) images. Stories, like paintings, are objects of perception, and their constituents can be referred to.

The way we use the word "real" can add to our confusion. We distinguish mental images from real images and real images from real things. The latter distinction can be easily clarified by examples. A cardboard pony is a real image; a pony is a real thing. A photograph of a tree is a real image; a tree is a real thing. And so on.

This chapter began by noting the collapse of Hilary Putnam's effort to save realism from the myth of the framework by replacing the intentional theory of reference with a causal theory of reference. Putnam's realism was doomed because he did not understand the autonomy of the observation framework and the tiered structure of the life framework, with the observation framework at its foundation. The sort of realism he wanted cannot, in my opinion, be defended without understanding these things. Putnam was barred from this understanding because he, like so many of his colleagues, had been smitten by an ideal mathematics. I have rehearsed at length the many effects of what I have called "the love affair with mathematics,'' and I have begun to describe the advantages that await us once the love affair is over.

In the next chapter I shall put forward a general view of knowledge and justification that properly takes into account the theory/observation distinction developed heretofore. This view of knowledge and justification will, of course, contrast sharply with the one typical of the myth of the framework, the so-called ''coherence theory'' of justification. The chapter will pull together much of the earlier argument and allow further reflection on the nature of the philosophical discussion we have been conducting.

Chapter VII

KNOWLEDGE AND JUSTIFICATION

In recent years the most generally accepted definition of knowledge has been "justified true belief." Two-thirds of this definition seems reasonably clear and acceptable. "Belief" is in many contexts contrasted with "knowledge." In this definition, however, it names a genus covering all states of at least minimal conviction, whether well founded or not, whether true or not. That such belief must be true to be classified as knowledge seems indisputable. But it is not enough for it to be true. A lucky guess that turns out true is not knowledge. What is needed in addition is that the belief be well founded or "justified." It is this third part of the definition that has been the least clear and the most controversial. Well-known Gettier counterexamples have illustrated some of the problems with it.[1] Suppose that my physician tells me that a lump on my neck is not malignant, and suppose that it's true that it's not malignant. Do I then know that the lump is not malignant? The belief is true and seems to be justified. But let's suppose my doctor mistakenly based his judgment upon a lab report that, in fact, concerned someone else's lump. The doctor's belief, though true, was unjustified; and my belief, based on the doctor's, was also un-

---

[1]Edmund Gettier, "Is Justified True Belief Knowledge?" *Analysis* 23:2 (February 1963): 121-23. For an excellent summary of the attempts to overcome Gettier-style objections to the "traditional" analysis of knowledge, see the "Introduction" in George Pappas and Marshall Swain, eds., *Essays on Knowledge and Justification* (Ithaca NY: Cornell University Press, 1978). These essays exemplify the heretofore main lines of response to Gettier and the problems with them.

justified. The example shows that a distinction must be made between real justification and apparent justification. This distinction means that there are two general ways that a person competently and sincerely claiming to know something can be wrong: (1) his belief may not be true, or (2) his belief may appear to be justified, but not really be justified. The exploration of this last distinction requires a more sophisticated statement of the meaning of "justification" than has prevailed up to now.

The two rival general approaches to justification in recent years have been coherence theories and foundational theories. Coherence theories are part of the myth of the framework and insist that all justification is circular. Foundational theories come in two versions—one associated with formal foundationalism, the other with informal foundationalism. Both insist that justification can or must have termini. The differences between the two foundationalisms were spelled out at the beginning of chapter five. Formal foundationalism, in its most stringent mathematical cast, insists upon absolutely certain termini for justification and upon reductive connections between these termini and any statement that is justified. Informal foundationalism denies both these tenets and opposes the theory of meaning that goes with them.[2] Full-scale formal foundationalism has by now been generally repudiated in the philosophical literature, although somewhat rearguard actions defending parts of the theory can still be found. Informal foundationalism is partly the brainchild of the present author, but it has many antecedents.[3] Coherence theory, on the third hand, has seemed to be the wave of the present.

Most of my argument against the coherence theory of justification and in favor of informal foundationalism is already in place. Coherence theory holds that all justification is circular, depending on the framework as a whole and not upon any privileged sort of knowledge upon which the framework is based. All apparently foundational statements—for example, observation statements—are themselves functions of the framework, as dependent upon it as it is upon them. Two physicists, for example, adhering to different theories may gaze into the cloud chamber and claim to see two

---

[2]See n. 4 below.

[3]Among the antecedents are Fred Dretske, "Conclusive Reasons"; James Cornman, "Foundational versus Nonfoundational Theories of Empirical Justification"; and Mark Pastin, "Modest Foundationalism and Self-Warrant," in Pappas and Swain, *Essays on Knowledge*.

different things. What each sees is a function of the theory he holds; it is not an independent basis for that theory.

In my earlier replies to such arguments I have distinguished between explaphors and terms from the autonomous observation framework. Explaphors are figures of speech and functions of theories of physics, astronomy, philosophy, theology, or whatever. They change when the theories change. Those who use explaphors in support of coherence theory depend on the rhetorical effect of missing this distinction and then making it appear that what can be said of explaphors can be said of observation terms in general. The distinction between explaphor and literal observation term shows this generalization to be a non sequitur. Words in the autonomous observation framework are definable in terms of one another and of their relationship to objects of observation. They do not depend upon the sorts of theories physicists gazing into cloud chambers may disagree about. Thus, the first part of my attack upon the coherence theory of justification is my argument for the existence of the autonomous observation framework. The existence of this framework pulls the stingers from the explaphors coherence theory has used to make the capture of observation by theories a *tour d'essaim.*

The second part of my attack is the defense of givenness. Not only are theories of physics, astronomy, and so on asymmetrically grounded by observation, the observation framework itself is grounded by the original givenness of the objects of observation. I explained earlier how prelinguistic awareness of medium-sized objects and their properties contributes in humans to the rise of the sort of observation framework we have. I did this to rebut Rorty's claim that prelinguistic awareness is irrelevant to all questions of justification. Rorty made this mistake because he overlooked the constitutive role prelinguistic awareness has in the first stages of concept formation, prior to any acts of justification. Granted that justification of beliefs must be expressed in language, as Rorty rightly insists, if the meaning of observational language as a whole is constituted by its connection with perceived observational givens, then such givens are part of the ultimate ground being appealed to when observation language is used to justify our beliefs. The observation framework is anchored downward to observational givens, not upward to the often transitory bursts of theory. This conclusion gives us what Russell, Moore, Husserl, and Dewey needed when they repudiated idealism early in this century, claiming it rode roughshod over the data of experience. Informal foundationalism returns observation to its privileged position in justifying our beliefs, but without adopting the mathematico-logical preoccupations that would set the whole empiricist-idealist dialectic in motion again.

Now that we have reviewed in summary fashion the general case for the informal foundationalist theory of justification, we can turn our attention in more detail to its application. Just as the life framework is a tiered framework with the observation framework at the bottom and the theoretical framework adjoined to it, so justification is of two general sorts: (1) justification of beliefs in the observation framework and (2) justification of beliefs in the theoretical framework. The parallels with my earlier discussion of reference to objects will become clear as we go.

1. The paradigm expression of justification in the autonomous observation framework is "I know it because I see it." (In what follows, I will use "see" for any sensory perception.) I know the lamp is lit, red, made of wood, because I see it is lit, red, made of wood. No further justification is necessary. If I am trying to persuade someone else that my belief is justified, the strongest evidence I can give is to let him see for himself. Justification by appeal to perception offers a way to distinguish between real and apparent justification. I may think I am seeing, hearing, touching something when, in fact, I am not doing so. Such seeing, hearing, touching provide no real justification; and beliefs based on them are not knowledge, no matter how convincing the deception. The physician who said, "I know the lump is not malignant because I saw the lab report on it"—and who actually saw only a lab report on something else—is not justified, though he thinks he is.

This is such an obvious reply to Gettier problems about justified true belief that one wonders why anyone thought there was a problem in the first place. The reason for the problem is that, according to the requirements of formal foundationalism, a *certain* (in the Cartesian sense) starting point for justification had to be found. This required that justification be based upon how things *appear,* since, it was thought, we cannot be wrong about how things appear to us. But if justification must be based upon how things appear, and how they appear is always certain, there is no possibility of a false or merely apparent justification. The *ap-*

pearances could not be false or merely apparent.[4] Thus, Gettier examples expose another breach in the armor of formal foundationalism, by sticking its theory of justification. The way to avoid the problem is to give up the formal foundationalist requirement of a certain (in the Cartesian sense) foundation. Once the foundation of justification is moved away from the appearances of things (sense data, and so on) to the perception of things, we can readily make the distinctions necessary to account for Gettier examples. This is exactly what informal foundationalism does.

It might seem, however, that distinguishing between true and false justifications leads to an infinite regress. It might seem that the foundational justification (paradigm: "because I see it") must itself be justified, requiring an answer to the question: How do I *know* that I see it? The problem with this question is that it cannot be answered by appeal to anything more justified than perception itself. And this is exactly the point of saying that perception, though fallible, is foundational. There is only one reasonable answer to the question, How do I know that I see it? By observing carefully and, perhaps, by having others do the same. There is nothing more to be done.

Even the coherence theorist admits that at this point justification is at an end. He just explains it differently. He claims that the end-statement describing what has been observed is a function of changeable theory. We have already seen why statements in the autonomous observation framework should not be so construed. Once the coherence theory's vision of the connection between theory and observation has been thrown out, what we have left are the fallible foundations for justification in perception that characterize informal foundationalism.

So far we have been discussing justifications of belief in the autonomous observation framework. What can we say about justifications that involve explaphors? Explaphors are functions of theories and are therefore justified only to the extent that the the parent theory is justified. They cannot be justified in terms of the observation framework alone. When the physics student feels the steel rod getting hot and says, "The molecular vibrations are being transmitted," his statement is no more justified than the theory

---

[4]For my disagreement with the Cartesian view that appearances are always certain, see my "Roderick Chisholm: Self and Others," *Review of Metaphysics* 33:1 (September 1979): 141-43. My views expressed there are not crucial for the present argument, however.

that says heat is molecular vibration. When theories are not well justified, both they and any statements using explaphors derived from them are, at best, what was classically called "opinion" to contrast it with "knowledge." Often a theory may be rather well justified, but some person using its explaphors may be simply accepting it uncritically and without justification. In the case of such a person, the acceptance of the theory is also a matter of "opinion," not knowledge. But now we are getting ahead of ourselves. To understand the justification of explaphors in observation, it is clear we must first understand the justification of theories.

2. Theories can be divided into two general categories, depending on the kind of justification available for them. These days the first kind are usually called "scientific theories." They make predictions that are sufficiently precise in a domain sufficiently controllable that we say they are "verified" if their predictions come true. These days theories of the second kind are usually called "metaphysical theories." Their predictions are insufficiently precise or their domains insufficiently controllable to be "verifiable" in anything but a vague way. As we shall see, it would be wrong to think of this second kind of theory as "unscientific" in a pejorative sense. It includes much of social science, as well as virtually all of philosophy, theology, and other beliefs people live by.

A theory is justified as a whole. Observation beliefs (except those using explaphors) can be justified one at a time. I can justify believing "the cat is on the mat" by seeing it there, without having to justify anything else. Understanding "the cat is on the mat" requires understanding many other expressions, but meaning and justification are not the same in this respect. The *meaning* of an observation statement depends in part upon its connection with other expressions in the observation framework. The *justification* of an observation statement does not depend upon the justification of other statements in the observation framework. It is true that justification of any one belief will always imply justification of many other actual or possible beliefs (for example, the cat is visible, the mat exists, and so on), but nothing need be said or thought concerning justification of any further belief in order for "the cat is on the mat" to be justified by seeing the cat there.

The same cannot be said of statements that are parts of theories. Their justification, for better or for worse, is hitched completely to the justification of the theory as a whole.[5] According to informal foundationalism, theory construction is an exercise in what might be called "creative insight." It is "creative" because it requires much more than just logical operations upon observation statements. It is "insight" because it is an attempt to get at the underlying causes of what is observed. In other words, observations serve as the inspiration for theory construction, but they do not control its course in strictly logical fashion. All theories worthy of the name, whether scientific or metaphysical, are products of creative insight. Scientific theories are a special case because they can be justified not only as products of attempted insight, but by the verification of their clear predictions.

To understand how belief in theories can be justified, it is first necessary to distinguish two kinds of belief about a theory's success: (1) belief that a theory works; (2) belief that a theory is true. A theory that is true will, of course, work, if properly applied; but a theory that works in some domain or other may not be true. The contrapositive follows: if a theory does not work, then something about it clearly is not true. It would therefore be unreasonable for anyone to believe that a theory is true and yet doesn't work. Such an unsuccessful theory is at best incomplete.

Pragmatists, of course, deny the distinction between the two different kinds of belief, claiming that we can never know more than that a theory works or doesn't work. Consequently we should understand "it's true" to mean "it works" and "it's false" to mean "it doesn't work"—and nothing more. In chapter 10 I will discuss this somewhat anomalous separation of realism and pragmatism in its historical context. For now, let me simply point out that the pragmatist redefinition of "truth" depends upon a denial of the givenness of foundational truth in the observation framework. If my defense of the latter has been successful, then the pragmatist identification of "it works" with "it's true" has already been shut out. Let's investigate further the usefulness of the distinction.

Failure to distinguish between "justified belief that a theory works" and "justified belief that a theory is true" causes the following problems. When we read the history of science, we are im-

---

[5]The only exception would be predictions that flow from a theory and are stated entirely in terms of the observation framework, with explaphors deleted. Such predictions lead the double life I described earlier: they function as part of a theory and as part of the autonomous observation framework and are a joining point between the two.

pressed with a sense that our brilliant intellectual ancestors were surely quite justified in holding most of the theories they did. Yet we know that many of those theories have more recently been contradicted and superseded. We feel caught in an uncomfortable trap and are not sure what to say. It seems arrogant and unfair to say that these brilliant predecessors of ours were simply unjustified in their beliefs, but it makes us us uncomfortable to say that they were justified, but wrong so much of the time. When our criteria for justification are so loose that a large proportion of justified beliefs within a certain category end up being false, we naturally think the criteria for that category should be tightened. It seems clear that a large proportion of past scientific theories were false. How then can we say that those who held them were justified?

The coherence theory of justification, as part of the myth of the framework, offers a way out of this quandary. We are told that our ancestors were wrong when judged from the perspective of the theories we hold today, but that they were right from their own perspective. The myth of the framework holds that truth is entirely a function of framework. According to our ancestors' frameworks, their scientific theories were right; according to ours, they were wrong.

This view of truth is, of course, as trivial as it sounds. Once again, however, we find that we do not have to go to this extreme to resolve conflicting loyalties to solid justification and to brilliant ancestors. Informal foundationalism solves the problem by making the distinction between different kinds of justified belief. The great scientists of the past were frequently justified in believing their theories would work; they were only rarely justified in believing their theories were true. It is not a great discredit to them that they were often mistaken about the kind or level of justification they had achieved. We are more aware of the vicissitudes of theory change than they were in a position to be. To construct theories that work well, even if they are eventually superseded by better ones, is no mean accomplishment. It is a worthy fruit of brilliant labor, and is seldom surpassed, even today. Presently held theories "work better," for the most part, than their predecessors; but for the great majority of them, we are justified only in believing they work well—even superbly—not that they are true. To justify belief that a theory is true, it must not only work superbly, provide a plausible and coherent causal model, and be consistent with equally confirmed theories; it must also make successful, novel predictions of a sort that would not have been expected except for the theory. This is the best possible indicator that creative insight has actually grasped something of the underlying mechanisms of the observable world.

If justified belief in the truth of *scientific* theories is so difficult, it might seem that justified belief in the truth of *metaphysical* theories is well-nigh impossible. This is perhaps a slight overstatement. It is true that precisely testable predictions give scientific theories a vehicle for justification that metaphysical theories lack, but all theories are products of attempted insight. If any theory is ever true, it is so because insight has succeeded. Can metaphysical insight succeed? I have already claimed that belief in the truth of a scientific theory can be justified. If I am right, then we are justified in saying that theoretical insight can at times arrive at the truth. But if this is so in the scientific domain, there seems no reason to think it is not so in the metaphysical domain. The two domains differ on verification procedures, but both depend on creative insight; and truth is the product of insight, not of verification procedures. Heliocentrism was true before it was verified. It was true because insight had hit the mark. Science has often been used to discredit metaphysics. I have used it here to support metaphysics. Science enables us to know that creative insight can bring us to the truth. It happens that most kinds of creative insight cannot be subjected to scientific verification. This does not prevent them from being true.

Granted this point about the truth of metaphysical theories, what about their justification? This, after all, was our original question. What could count as a justification? We have already distinguished the method of metaphysics from the method of science. Let's call the method of metaphysics by the traditional name "dialectic." Dialectical reasoning, lacking appeal to experimental confirmation, is a kind of *via negativa.* It is far more a process of rejecting positions than of affirming them. Theories are rigorously sifted for their consistency. Their implications are drawn out and compared with one another. Progress is made by eliminating some of the alternatives—by exposing their inconsistencies, reducing them to absurdity, showing them to be trivial or meaningless, and so on. Once we are satisfied, using these methods, that some theories are untenable, we begin to think we are justified in believing the truth lies among the remaining alternatives.

The typical pitfalls of dialectical method are not only mistaken or "strawman" criticisms of theories, but also the fallacy of incomplete alternatives and the positing of overly definite conclusions. The fallacy of incomplete alternatives is a conclusion from the falsity of A and B to the truth of F, without considering C, D, and E. The positing of overly definite conclusions is similar. It results from forgetting that the method is largely a *via negativa* that usually leaves a broad remainder. The fallacy lies in arriving at conclusions gratuitously narrower than this remainder. My earlier criticism of standard materialism and dualism claimed that both sides hold overly definite conclusions that cannot be justified or even well sustained by the relevant dialectical arguments. My criticism of the myth of the framework has been, broadly speaking, twofold. The dialectic to the myth commits the fallacy of incomplete alternatives by thriving on its attack of formal foundationalism and correspondence theory, but without considering informal foundationalism. I have worked to show that the latter is not defeated by such or similar attacks. Secondly, I have attacked the myth of the framework directly as inconsistent with the foundational role perception actually plays in our coming to know.

It seems to me that dialectical reasoning in the hands of very skilled thinkers who avoid the pitfalls and are capable of great insight can lead to justified belief. This does not happen easily, and very few are capable of it. But we dare not give up the effort for all that. Indeed, most, if not all, of the central issues of life lie within the metaphysical domain. Our scientific, political, moral, cultural, and religious thinking rest upon dialectical reasoning and metaphysical insight. During one high water mark of formal foundationalism, the disciples of Saint-Simon believed this whole metaphysical realm of dialectical conversation could be replaced by science. Scientists, especially social scientists, would give us the right answers to all questions about how we should conduct ourselves. This vain expectation should seem ludicrous to us today. Science itself is not nearly so sure-handed as the Saint-Simonians assumed. Social theory is more metaphysical than scientific; and, indeed, the "law of history" and "law of progress," which were to the Saint-Simonians paradigms of scientific law, were not only products of metaphysical reasoning, but metaphysical reasoning of a very questionable sort. Metaphysical pursuits can neither be replaced nor avoided. And if metaphysical knowledge seems so difficult that it can be achieved only rarely and by exceptional people, then at least some consensus of opinion on values, institutions, and the nature of man is needed for a political society to have unity and to prosper. I will say more about this in the next chapter; but before we move on, I would like to make two additional comments, the first very short and the second longer.

Religious belief, when it is the result of reasoning at all, emanates from metaphysical reasoning. Many religions have had the epistemological sophistication to recognize the difficulties involved in pursuing this sort of reasoning successfully. They speak of a special sort of enlightenment required to arrive at the relevant creative insight. And so Christians, for example, believe the foundational insight that God has communicated with mankind in specific revelational ways can be achieved only with the help of the Holy Spirit. This belief is perfectly consistent with the view that many people are Christians from acculturation rather than from insight; but it does implicitly acknowledge the difficulty of the insight, if there is to be any, from a natural point of view.

Finally, I would like to discuss Richard Rorty's distinction between "systematic" and "edifying" philosophers in light of what I've said about metaphysical reasoning. According to Rorty, systematic philosophers are people like Aristotle, Aquinas, Descartes, Kant, Hegel, Russell, and Husserl. Rorty regards their work as "essentially constructive"—the bulk of it presents a positive view of what the world is like or how we should think about it. Edifying philosophers are people like the later Wittgenstein, the later Heidegger, Nietzsche, Kierkegaard, and Sartre. Their work is "essentially reactive" rather than constructive. Rorty says some very curious-sounding things about these edifying philosphers. He says they present no arguments and have no views.[6] They "have to decry the very notion of having a view, while avoiding having a view about having views. . . . This is an awkward, but not impossible position."[7]

Why does Rorty think this is not impossible? It must be remembered that he makes these remarks in the final chapter of *Philosophy and the Mirror of Nature.* By then he has firmly ensconced himself in the myth of the framework and pulled up the ladder. The curious things he says about "edifying philosophers" show how they look from that vantage point. According to the myth of the framework, truth is entirely relative to framework. "To present a view" of how things actually are or "to argue" for or against the

[6]Richard Rorty, *Philosophy and the Mirror of Nature* (Princeton: Princeton University Press, 1979) 369, 372.

[7]Ibid., 371.

truth of something is not an activity that makes sense within the myth. What one does instead is make fun of such efforts. This, according to Rorty, is what edifying philosophers do. They are the heroes of the myth because they prevent the illusion that *any* view could be true or justified by arguement from getting too strong a hold. They do this, according to Rorty, without presenting any view of their own, nor do they argue that the views of systematic philosophers are untrue. This would require producing evidence against the truth of these views. But since, according to the myth, truth is entirely a function of one's framework, there can be no independent evidence either for or against truth. Therefore, edifying philosophers cannot argue against the truth of systematic philosophies—they just poke fun at their pretensions.

Now this is all very satisfactory for those who have joined Rorty inside the myth of the framework. For those of us who have not, however, there is another way of drawing the distinction between "systematic" and "edifying" philosophers. Dialectical or metaphysical reasoning has two moments, one critical and the other constructive. Virtually all philosphers, including the systematic ones, start their discussions by entertaining various received views and criticizing them. Most philosophers, including most of the edifying ones, do this with some notion, at least, of what a better alternative would look like. Socrates seems the clearest case of an exception to this last rule. He repeatedly ends discussions (to be continued on another day . . .) after attacking many received alternatives, but without presenting any positive doctrine. Because he proposes nothing, Socrates is never guilty of the fallacy of incomplete alternatives or of the fallacy of overly definite conclusions. He never claims to have considered all the alternatives, and his "conclusions" are so indefinite as to be hardly worthy of the name. One could say he has attempted to narrow the range of acceptable options, but without embracing any specific one. Even so, and spare as they are, Socrates' arguments can be evaluated as critiques. He gives us no positive doctrine to criticize, but he does give us critiques to criticize.

Other philosophers were more ambitious and did propose and defend positive doctrines. Some did this extensively. Aristotle, Plotinus, Aquinas, Kant, and Hegel are clear examples of systematic philosophers. Others did it much less extensively and appear to stay closer to the Socratic model. Although I do not intend to argue the point here, I disagree with Rorty's claim that Nietzsche, later Heidegger, later Wittgenstein, and Sartre had no positive doctrine. I grant that their positive doctrine is vague and unsystematic when compared to that of the first group of philosophers. This second group we can call "edifying" philosophers, if we wish; but the difference between them and the first group seems only a matter of degree. Both groups heavily employ the critical argumentation characteristic of the *via negativa.* One tries to supply an extensive alternative to the views it criticizes; the other, by and large, neglects or refuses to do so. The work of both groups can be used in later reconstructions of philosophical dialectic.

Perhaps the best way to evaluate Rorty's claim that edifying philosophers make no arguments and present no views is to scrutinize *Philosophy and the Mirror of Nature,* which Rorty regards as an exercise in edification. Using my own categories for the analysis of metaphysical discussion, I would say the book is full of critical arguments against, for example, formal foundationalism, correspondence theory, mind/body dualism, and so on. The positive doctrine that Rorty proposes is the myth of the framework, which depends upon the successful execution of a lengthy dialectic. I have charged that Rorty's dialectic commits the fallacy of incomplete alternatives and that the myth of the framework, like its idealist precursors, is inconsistent with the actual function of perception in our coming to know. If we apply to Rorty's book his own description of edifying philosophy, that it makes no arguments and presents no views, it follows that I have missed the point entirely because, on this assumption, he was not arguing against correspondence theory, and so on; he was only poking fun at them! Nor was he presenting the myth of the framework as his view! But the only way to make sense of such claims is to say that Rorty, from the start, assumed the myth of the framework. He was neither presenting it as a view nor arguing for it dialectically. He was just showing us at book length how one acts when one has already adopted the myth.

In reply to this Rortyan analysis of Rorty's book, I can only say the following. If Rorty has presented a dialectical argument for the myth of the framework, I have criticized and will further criticize that argument. If Rorty has merely assumed the myth of the framework, I have criticized and will further criticize that assumption. The *tertium quid* that will not be allowed is that Rorty sally forth to argue against other positions and then hide in the pillow of the myth to avoid being argued against in turn. Now, if Rorty were to say that from his viewpoint no arguments are allowed, and therefore, a priori, no arguments against the myth of the framework are allowed, then I shall be content to reply: Let all those who reject this move as insipidly self-serving line up with me. It is surely we who shall be able to carry on the conversation using the fullest range of conversational tools, including arguments.

This conclusion is tentative for now. In the next chapter we shall discuss the meaning of "toleration." Non-argumentativeness can assume the high moral ground of "tolerance" and make dialectical argument seem "intolerant" by comparison. The political hope associated with the myth of the framework is to establish, through acceptance of the myth, an ambience of toleration and individual freedom. This hope is a continuation of similar hopes expressed by the British writers Locke, Hume, and Oakeshott. If the spirit of toleration we desire is better served by the myth of the framework than by informal foundationalism, this advantage might attract us to accept it, despite its lack of congency in other respects. In any event, pursuing epistemological implications into ethics, politics, and the arts, as we shall do in the following chapters, will enable us to draw out some of the hidden agenda that can deeply influence our epistemological views, even if our view is that we should avoid having such views. Perhaps Aristotle, Dewey, and Rorty would agree with me that this hidden agenda deserves to be addressed.

Chapter VIII

TOLERATION

The notion that epistemological skepticism could be used to support pleas for religious and political toleration achieved currency in the late seventeenth century through the writings of Pierre Bayle and John Locke. The myth of the framework, because it denies any legitimate meaning for "truth" that is not framework relative, can be used in the same kinds of arguments for toleration. In this chapter we shall examine this connection between toleration and skepticism to see whether a case can be made for the myth of the framework by praising its support of toleration.

Pierre Bayle argued in 1686 that since all theories about the ultimate nature of reality are questionable, and since true belief cannot be distinguished from false belief, there cannot possibly be any justification for persecuting people for their beliefs.[1] The trouble with Bayle's argument is that, given his skeptical premises, there is not only no justification for persecution, there is no justification for any opinion or action whatever—including the opinion that persecution is wrong or should not be allowed and including any action taken to prevent it. Undoubtedly Bayle assumed that the burden of proof lay on the side of those condoning persecution. But this assumption cannot be supported in terms of his complete skepticism. It seems, rather, that his skeptical arguments *as such* can decide nothing, either for or against toleration. Only when the skeptical premises are coupled with

---

[1]Pierre Bayle, *Commentaire philosophique sur ces paroles de Jésus-Christ "Constrains-les d'entrer"* (Amsterdam: 1686).

additional reasoning that shows the burden of proof to rest upon the persecutors does the conclusion for toleration follow. The problem is to find additional reasoning that is consistent with the skeptical premises. Later we shall ask whether "convention" can be used as the missing ingredient.

In his "Introduction" to the Bobbs-Merrill edition of John Locke's *A Letter Concerning Toleration,* Patrick Romanell observes that "the fundamental assumption on which ultimately rests not only his (Locke's) case for religious tolerance but also his general philosophical position . . . (is) the limitation of the human mind." Locke "attacks 'the principle of persecution for religion' on the ground of human fallibility." Because religious views are fallible, "nobody has a right to *impose* them on others."[2] An argument for toleration based on fallibilism makes at least one of the following two assumptions:

(1) If I am strong in my convictions or think that I know something, I am thereby rendered intolerant, that is, I am inclined to persecute those who do not share my knowledge or conviction;
(2) If I am fallibilist or skeptical about belief, I will thereby be rendered tolerant, that is, I will tend to refrain from persecuting those who do not share my beliefs.

It seems to me that both of these assumptions are clearly false.

When one group persecutes another for its religious or other beliefs, it does so not simply because it has *any* convictions or claims to have *any* knowledge, but because it has *specific* convictions that seem immediately to justify persecution. Religious persecutors, for example, typically espouse one of the following justifying premises:

(1) Persecution will save the state from greater evils, such as:
    (a) God's wrath upon the society for its infidelity;
    (b) an anarchic breakdown of the unity required for effective government caused by plurality of religions or philosophies.

A person of the strongest religious convictions could believe that persecuting others will not contribute these benefits to society or to the state.

[2]Patrick Romanell, "Introduction," in John Locke, *A Letter Concerning Toleration* (Indianapolis: Bobbs-Merrill, 1955) 7.

(2) Persecution will save those persecuted from greater evils, such as:
   (a) violation of their most solemn oaths and promises, for example, those made at baptism;
   (b) the loss of their immortal souls.

Once again it seems posible for a person of strong religious conviction to deny that persecution is likely to confer these benefits upon those persecuted and to assert, to the contrary, that it is far more likely to confer great harm.

Indeed, Locke himself discusses all of these premises for persecution and gives reasons for denying each one of them. But once these and other specific pro-persecution premises are denied, it is possible for someone to have strong convictions, religious or otherwise, and to claim to have knowledge that many others lack, without desiring to persecute them. The case against persecution and intolerance is adequately made by attacking these pro-persecution premises. A general attack upon all conviction or knowledge is not necessary.

Nor is a general denial of all conviction or knowledge a sufficient condition for toleration. A skeptic or fallibilist might reason in the following way: "There is no way to tell who is right in these religious or political matters; so I might as well impose my own views by force, if I can." In other words, pro-persecution premises are as available to the skeptic as they are to the convinced religionist. The skeptic too may believe that the unity of the state requires singleness of framework and may persecute to achieve it. Or he may simply decide he is involved in a *bellum omnium contra omnes* and that such persecution serves the cause of his own hegemony and that of his group. Once again we arrive at the point we reached more quickly discussing Pierre Bayle: skepticism provides no justification for persecution nor any check upon it.

The two edges of the sword of skepticism have been displayed in the separate analyses of modern totalitarian thought offered by Bertrand Russell and Karl Popper,[3] and in the responses they engendered. Both Russell and Popper named various metaphysicians, and especially Hegel, as the intellectual sources of Nazism and Communism. Both believed a high degree of metaphysical skepticism to be the necessary antidote for these dangerous and

---

[3]Bertrand Russell, *The History of Western Philosophy* (New York: Simon and Schuster, 1946) 742. Karl Popper, *The Open Society and Its Enemies* (London: Routledge and Sons, 1945) Chapter 12.

destructive ideologies. Not only were Popper and Russell guilty of overgeneralization by indicting numerous metaphysicians who have no historical connection with the rise of any totalitarian state; even their central case of Hegel's connection with the rise of National Socialism does not stand scrutiny. During the period from 1918 on, Hegel's philosophy was out of favor in Germany, just as it was in England and in the United States. Hence it is difficult to derive historically the fervor of Nazism from worshipful Hegelianism. In fact, Leo Strauss and others have argued exactly the opposite way. They point out that the interbellum period in Germany had been characterized, not by metaphysical faith, but by skeptical despair. It was the *lack* of conviction and knowledge that made Germany an unresisting vacuum into which Hitler's vision could be poured. My point here is not that Strauss was clearly and completely right in his historical analysis, but that his observations about the possible effects of general skepticism are as valid as Locke's and Bayle's more sanguine ones. Skepticism seems a two-edged feather rather than sword: it neither persecutes nor defends against persecution.

The skeptic does, however, have one further defense against persecution that would appear to be consistent with his skepticism: convention. David Hume felt compelled to believe many things, despite his rather total epistemological skepticism. He could find no external ground—no God, no natural law—to explain the firmness of his convictions. He therefore found an internal, psychological ground—what today we might call the capacity of the human being to be conditioned. He thought of our strongest convictions as the results of our strongest conditioning. Thus, for example, my conviction that striking a bell causes it to ring is the result of my frequent perception that the bell rings each time it is struck. Because of this concomitance, I am conditioned to expect the bell to ring when it is struck. It is this conditioned expectation and nothing more that I express when I say that striking the bell causes it to ring.

In the political and moral domains, the conditioning apparatus takes the form of customs and traditions. We become moral and political beings insofar as we imbibe the customs and traditions of our forebears. There is nothing more to be said. Hume himself, for example, had imbibed the British tradition of the rights of Englishmen, Scot though he was; and because of this conditioning, he was a splendidly tolerant man. Also because of this conditioning, he desired to promote toleration in society as a whole and to make sure that the next generation would be conditioned to tolerance as well. Preserving toleration and other moral and political values was for Hume a matter of preserving the traditions and customs that inculcate these values. The meaning of "virtue" is defined by this conditioning tradition, and the virtuous are those who have successfully absorbed the lessons of "enculturation."

Two comments are in order. First, it is clear from what has been said that Hume is tolerant because of his convictions and not because of his skepticism. It is true that Hume believes his convictions to be grounded in such things as habit, custom, and tradition; but they are convictions nonetheless. Hume is tolerant because he is convinced that one should be tolerant, and he is convinced that one should be tolerant because, he says, he was brought up to think that way. Because of his skepticism, he can find no other basis for his convictions. But is someone who arrives at the same convictions by another, less skeptical, route any less tolerant? Mill was convinced that toleration was the best policy because of its utility in promoting the greatest good of the greatest number. Others favor toleration because they think it allows for the full flourishing of individual and communal goods, still others because they hold some theory of natural rights. And so on. Such theorists are less skeptical than Hume and less dependent upon sheer habit and custom than he is; does this make them and those who agree with them less tolerant, for all that? Once we have clearly seen that it is specific convictions that render us either tolerant or intolerant, the answer will be plain to us: skepticism is not, as such, an aid to toleration. Those who are far less skeptical than Hume can be among the most tolerant.

How then arose the myth that skepticism is synonymous with tolerance? Because philosophy took a skeptical turn in the late seventeenth and early eighteenth centuries, it became fashionable to use skeptical arguments to attack belief in pro-persecution premises. This attack works well enough when pro-persecution premises are based upon claims to know, and it happened that most pro-persecution premises were defended on just such a basis at that time. But when pro-persecution premises are based upon sheer pragmatism and/or desire for personal or group aggrandizement, such skeptical attacks are quite useless. Persecutors of the latter ilk are entirely comfortable with skepticism: they may be skilled at using it to confound their critics. If skepticism had not been the fashion at the turn of the eighteenth century, pro-persecution premises based on knowledge claims might just as well have been countered with anti-persecution premises based on knowledge claims, with no general skepticism on either side of the argument. The advantage of thus basing toleration upon positive argument is that such argument can then be turned in both directions, to defend against both kinds of persecutors: (a) those who say they know (pro-persecution premises) and (b) those who say they know not, but who choose to seek hegemony by using force to limit others. In retrospect, we can see that the skeptical attack upon intolerance helped give skepticism a high moral sheen it would have otherwise lacked. The attack upon intolerance just at a time when the intellectuals of Europe felt continuously threatened by religious persecution made skepticism respectable. This respectability seems somewhat an historical accident, and conferring such respectability upon the heir apparent myth of the framework is to perpetuate that accident uncritically. Perhaps the previous discussion has made clear to what the myth of the framework is actually heir.

My second comment on Hume's use of convention to base his view of toleration starts with a question: What if it is the custom to be intolerant? This seems a blithely simpleminded question, but its irony is even greater than might at first appear. It is curious that skepticism should be forced back upon convention to ground its case against intolerance, for the case against intolerance was in the first place an attack upon convention. Religious intolerance had, after all, become customary through virtually all of Europe. Locke attacked and suffered from the practice of religious persecution. Indeed, the entire skeptical tradition of the seventeenth and eighteenth centuries aimed its most powerful guns against traditional ways of thinking: what Bacon called "idols." This is not difficult to understand when the purpose is to clear the ground to set inquiry on the secure path of science as Bacon, Descartes, Kant, and others conceived it. Their attacks upon convention were meant to uncover a ground other than convention, a true ground.

Hume took a very different path, however. His one truth was that all moral knowledge is a matter of psychology and convention. The convention that he would sweep away is the conventional belief that there is something more than convention upon which our beliefs can be founded, some objective truth or objective morality. Hume realized it is madness to question everything at once; and so he cheerfully allowed his blind spots to be filled with conventional thinking, even as he focused his attention upon one or the other part of the tradition that he wished at the moment to call into question. But most of the tradition never got questioned and so functioned as the platform, the vantage point, from which Hume's world was seen and his skeptical excursions launched.

One wonders which is more central to Hume's thinking: his convictions based upon some parts of tradition or his skeptical attacks upon other parts of tradition. Does he really believe his greatest convictions are based on nothing more than conditioning? Or is this just his urbane way of justifying his practice of believing some things so firmly? If we take him at his word that he needs both wings in order to fly, both traditional dogmatism and anti-traditional skepticism, then we are amazed at what different flights two such wings can produce. Suppose one chose, unlike Hume, to cast skeptical doubt upon the practice of toleration and to leave unquestioned the practice of religious persecution. One would still be in full flight on the Humean wings, tradition on one side, skepticism on the other.

Once we recognize that it was the chief aim of skepticism, including Hume's, to call traditional ways of thinking into question, it soon dawns on us that the choice of which traditions to doubt and which traditions to leave unquestioned looks, from the skeptical point of view, like nothing more than arbitrary choice. Hume, it turns out, simply decided (perhaps unreflectively) to be tolerant rather than not. He might have been intolerant and been no less conventional and skeptical than he was. Even when we presuppose a tradition of respect for individual liberties such as prevailed in Hume's Britain, adherence to tradition combined with skepticism of it offers little dependable support for such liberties. We shall return in chapter nine to the ineluctable threat skepticism poses to traditional culture.

If the problem is this great for the skeptic's defense of toleration when a tradition of individual liberty is presupposed, the defense seems to evaporate when no such tradition exists. Voltaire chided Hume that it was all very well for him to rest his case for individual liberty on custom—England had such customs to defend and perpetuate, while eighteenth century France did not. In France those who aspired to champion anything resembling the rights of Englishmen did so by satirizing the unlibertarian conventions of the *ancien régime* and by promoting ideas of equality and dignity based on human nature. The writings of Rousseau and Voltaire offer numerous examples of the appropriate genre. Two things are, for my purposes, noteworthy about this contrast between Britain and France: (1) If Hume's conservatism were applied in France, it would have worked against toleration and individual liberty, the customs being what they were in France. (2) Voltaire, Rousseau, and other Frenchmen applied their skepticism to the conventions of the day in France, romanticizing the return to a pure creational starting point from which to embark freshly and nakedly again. They combined skepticism and conviction in a way opposite from Hume. They upheld the tradition of a morality based upon human nature (which Hume skeptically rejected), and sought to overthrow the customs of eighteenth century France (while Hume rested his entire morality upon the customs of Great Britain). It is not clear from a study of Hume's skeptical conservatism how exactly, in his view, his counterparts in France went wrong.

It is clear, however, that two heirs of Hume's conservatism, Edmund Burke and Michael Oakeshott, using hindsight during and after the French Revolution, were convinced that Hume's contemporaries in France did go wrong. Michael Oakeshott directed his skeptical barbs primarily at what he called "rationalisms," political philosophies that start from Bacon's first rule of inquiry: to lay aside received opinion and "begin anew from the very foundations."[4] Oakeshott called these "ideologies" and "abstractions," showing a philosophical dependence that goes beyond Hume to Hegel. An abstraction is, for Oakeshott, a partial image of the world, valid within limited contexts, that is absolutized and extrapolated beyond its range of validity. Such ideologues as Rousseau and Voltaire do not, in Oakeshott's opinion, take into account the concreteness of political life. They fail to understand that we must always begin both reflection and reform *in medias res:* there is no pristine starting point to be revisited. The main effect of pretending such a starting point is to undermine the traditions of behavior that constitute our political and moral existence. We must start from this tradition of behavior, not to dispense with it, but to accept it with appreciation. Only then can we set about improving our situation with any hope of success—by "amending existing arrangements to make them more coherent."[5]

---

[4]Michael Oakeshott, *Rationalism in Politics* (New York: Basic Books, 1962) 15.

[5]Ibid., 21.

Oakeshott's "politics of repair" resembles Edmund Burke's politics of "gradual improvement." The main difference is that Burke's ideas embodied an explicit Christian pessimism. This pessimism led him to view with distrust rationalist philosophies advocating revolution. These he called "abstractions," as Oakeshott did later. To him they were theories of progress that attempt to deny the human limitation and sin resulting from the Fall. They would sweep aside all of tradition as if man were about to save himself from his earthly condition. Rather, Burke believed, we should appreciate the hard-won good of our traditions and work to minimize the evils that always remain. If, instead, we destroy these traditions, we will destroy the best check we have upon the darkest side of human malice, ignorance, prejudice, and so on, which are an inevitable part of human nature in the present dispensation. Burke viewed the Revolution in France as just such an unleashing of the darkest side of human nature. As an Englishman he would have found the situation in pre-Revolutionary France stifling to his cherished liberties, but nevertheless he advocated the course of gradual improvement, slow as it might be, as the best hope for genuine improvement.

Like Hume and Oakeshott, Burke was a conservative, but they would have been skeptical of his appeal to Christianity and to Christian natural law. Burke had a positive basis for his case against intolerance that went beyond convention. He defended tradition, not because he thought it the entire causal source of moral values, but because it was the chief instrument for controlling the immoral viciousness that had its source in human sin and that violated a prior standard found in God's Commandments and human nature. Oakeshott gives the purer inheritance from Hume: he appears content to base his political philosophy upon skepticism on the one hand and convention on the other. Let's see if Oakeshott progresses beyond Hume in handling the problems of this position.

It may seem that Oakeshott made progress in handling the intolerance that arises from rationalist ideologies, showing exactly why the skeptic rejects these ideologies. According to Oakeshott, Rousseau and Voltaire were wrong because they attempted to strip away all tradition and custom, the accreted chains of civilization, and find beneath them the original innocence of nature. Skeptical sarcasm can be heaped upon the existence of such a nature, its innocence, and the possibility of forming it anew and doing it right this time. From the viewpoint of skeptical conservatism, the problem with thinkers who follow Bacon's first rule is that they usually end up claiming they have discovered a starting point prior to custom and outside tradition. It is not just that they choose to keep a romantic natural law tradition and to discard the *ancien régime.* They are not choosing among traditions as Hume did at all. They think this nature business is the "real stuff," not just another tradition. It is this edging outside the bounds of tradition that a skeptic like Oakeshott would stomp.

But to say that the rightness of human liberties depends upon something other than custom had been the customary way of putting it. To say they depend only upon custom and tradition was neither customary nor traditional. Who then was daring to edge his way outside the tradition, Rousseau or Hume? It seems both of them were and were not. But then we seem back to the problem of arbitrary choice among traditions. How can the skeptic show that his choice of which convention to follow and which to junk is better than someone else's choice?

Oakeshott addresses this question by drawing on the dialectical thought of Kant and Hegel. This procedure raises two issues: whether his own formulation of this dialectical thought is viable and whether his use of it requires that he go beyond skepticism and convention.

Within the domain of practical activity, Oakeshott believes the world can be seen *sub specie voluntatis* and *sub specie moris.*[6] What he means by "voluntatis" is very close to Schopenhauer's meaning of "will" understood as desire. Accordingly, my praxis is ruled, in the first place, by my desires. What is to keep me, if I am a skeptic, from attempting to impose my desires on others and trying to manipulate them to satisfy myself and my group? What is to keep me, to return to the leitmotif of this chapter, from being intolerant of people and ideas that stand in the way of my full gratification?

Oakeshott says that the check upon desire is found in the vision of the world *sub specie moris.* ("Moris" has a convenient ambiguity, meaning both "custom" and "morality.") This second vision is the result of deontological reflection, my recognition of others as loci of desires just like my own. Once this is recognized, so the argument goes, reason alone (that is, consistency alone) requires that I see the desires of others to be as valid as my own and

---

[6]Ibid., 209.

treat others as ends in themselves and not merely as means to my own gratification. Earlier I argued that while skepticism provides no justification for persecution, it likewise provides no check upon it. Perhaps deontology can fill this gap, offering a way to counter intolerance and persecution that neither skepticism nor convention alone could provide. If this can be done solely on the grounds of consistency, it would seem to avoid importing anything alien into skeptical conservatism. This, however, is exactly the issue: Is a deontological ethic merely a matter of applied consistency, or does it require metaphysical assumptions that the skeptical conservative cannot grant?

Let's examine closely the deontological reasoning proposed above. It is a fact that each one of us has desires. It would be a curious kind of misunderstanding for me not to recognize that others have desires just as I do. But what does it mean to make the further judgment that the desires of others "are as valid as" my own? What does "valid" mean here? It does not mean simply "real" or "factual." To say that the desires of others are as real or as factual as my own does not require that I should take these desires into account when they conflict with my own. The fact that others have desires may serve only to warn me that I will have to overcome others in order to satisfy my own desires. What does it mean to say that my own desires are "valid"?—that they are "good?"—that they are "not bad?" If I claim that my own desires are good, then consistency would require me to admit that relevantly similar desires in others are just as good as my own. But on what grounds do I claim that my desires are not only a fact of my existence, but also good? This seems to require some sort of clandestine natural law reasoning—the sort of reasoning that skeptics do not accept. Can we base this claim that my desires are good on convention? But then we have returned to the problem we boarded deontology to solve: the problem of showing that choice among conventions, is, for a skeptic, not merely arbitrary.

Perhaps we must drop this whole effort at a deontological solution and return to Hobbes. Hobbes does not import evaluative expressions that contradict his own skeptical moral positivism. He insists that we accept the laws that place limits upon the gratification of our own desires for, in fact, only one reason: fear. We fear lawless chaos and so we submit to a ruler; and then we fear the ruler and so we submit to his laws. But see how far short this falls from what the skeptical conventionalist hoped to achieve.

Toleration and respect for individual rights were hardly essential features of Hobbesian justice.

Oakeshott has one move left. He can try to mine the Hegelian lode that we glimpsed when he called "rationalisms" forms of "abstraction." To say that a political theory is an abstraction is to say that it is not "whole"—it leaves out altogether or fails to integrate important considerations necessary for completeness. At any time in its history, a given society is also incomplete, not a perfect whole. According to Oakeshott, the politics of repair discovers these points of incompleteness by noticing inconsistencies in current arrangements. As these inconsistencies are faced and overcome, the society progresses. Once again the procedure seems to promise the skeptical conventionalist help in solving his problems. He could use "holism" to show that the choice between conventions is not merely arbitrary. He can direct the politics of repair to discover which conventions can be integrated into a consistent larger whole and which are inconsistent with such higher integration. It would only remain for him to show that toleration and respect for individual liberties are more coherent in this holistic sense than are their alternatives. Thus, by a test of coherence alone, the skeptical conventionalist could rally a defense of these liberal values.

One more than suspects, however, that this procedure involves not only tests for coherence, but also visions of what sorts of "wholes" one wants to establish. Indeed, when one reads Hegel, Marx, or Oakeshott as they analyze the past in terms of historical dialectic, it is clear that for each there is a teleology operative. This may be fine for Hegel and even Marx, who are both explicitly metaphysical in their thinking. It is not so fine for those who see Oakeshott as a champion of skeptical conventionalism.

In "The Masses in Representative Democracy,[7]" Oakeshott describes how the notion of individual freedom "emerged" in medieval times, when the individual began to escape from communal and other established pressures. This Oakeshott sees as an immensely favorable development. He then describes the rise of the "anti-individual" as part of the reversion from "parliamentary" to "popular" government. This he sees as an immensely unfavorable development. But it seems clear from the text that he is

[7]Michael Oakeshott, "The Masses in Representative Democracy," in Albert Hunold, ed., *Freedom and Serfdom* (Dordrecht, Netherlands: D. Reidel, 1961).

not basing these judgments for and against on arguments from internal consistency. He is just extremely fond of the English system. It defines the "whole" in terms of which he judges the "consistency" of its predecessors and of contemporary competitors. This is conventionalism coupled with a Whiggish reading of the past and present so as to place the English parliamentary system at the apex of an historical arc. But this gerrymandering of past and present offers scant protection for toleration and individual liberties because it is a game any number can play. Just as the rejection of the communal pressures of the medieval period can be seen as an advance from the perspective of the "whole" of parliamentary liberty, so the rejection of parliamentary liberty can be seen as an advance from the perspective of the "whole" of totalitarian cooperation. Oakeshott does not like the rise of the "anti-individual," but on his own principles there is no way to distinguish his resistance of this new wave from the medieval conservative's resistance of individual liberty.

It appears, then, that recourse to deontological and dialectical reasoning cannot mitigate the thoroughgoing arbitrariness of the skeptical conventionalist's defense of toleration and individual liberties. As we saw earlier in this chapter, it is not skepticism but conviction that must serve as the basis for toleration. If conviction is based on conditioning alone, it seems the arbitrary effect of whoever has the power to condition. If skepticism typically calls into question some traditional ways of thinking while leaving others, for the time being, unquestioned, the decision which tradition to attack and which to leave in peace also seems arbitrary. Toleration as a custom might be preserved or discontinued, depending on what one's skepticism is targeting at any given time.

The point of this chapter thus far has been to press the debate between the myth of the framework and informal foundationalism into the ethical and political domains. I conceded at the beginning that if political toleration and individual liberties could be better maintained under the assumptions of the myth than under those of informal foundationalism, this would argue for the myth. We can see, however, that this is not the case. Informal foundationalism allows a positive case for toleration. Toleration, as I have repeated often, is based on conviction, not skepticism. Granted the indispensable role of tradition and custom for reinforcing convictions and educating each new generation, there seem to be clear advantages and no disadvantages to finding more ultimate foundations for these convictions than the simple fact that certain customs and traditions exist. This last point will be discussed at greater length in the next chapter.

Before ending this chapter, I would like to make a final comment on Rorty's contention that "edifying philosophers" like himself have no views and make no arguments. I argued earlier that to make this claim in the strong sense, Rorty must assume from the start that the myth of the framework is correct. If he did not assume it is correct, he would then have to argue for it and present it as his view. If he assumes it is correct, he need do neither—unless, of course, he chooses to defend himself against those who attack this assumption. But he could refuse to get involved in any argument whatever and simply play the pied piper, inviting people to accept his view of things. I have been hard at work trying to expose the hidden enticements that might lure people into doing just that. One of these enticements is the fact that "having no views and making no arguments" also has a weak sense. I believe Rorty means it in the strong sense given above because he needs the strong sense to avoid the charge that he is doing philosophy even as he tries to put an end to philosophy, thus invigorating it contrary to all his intentions. The weak sense is far more plausible than the strong sense, and confusion of the two can increase the attractiveness of what Rorty says about his "edifying philosophy."

The weak sense of these expressions is the following: (1) "Giving no arguments" means "giving no arguments of the sort employed by formal foundationalism." To give no arguments in this sense would be to eschew the formal foundationalist project of reductive definitions of all knowledge in terms of discrete perceptibles. The informal foundationalist would also claim to "give no arguments" in this sense, which is simply to repudiate formal foundationalism. (2) "Having no views" means, in the weak sense, "in principle, never being unwilling to consider new, cogent, and relevant evidence." Once again the informal foundationalist, who admits to a creative component in the process of theory construction, is ready to have this creative component tested by evidence. Those who, like formal foundationalists, deny or deplore this creative component are more likely to think they have no need for further checks once the argument has been carried through "clearly and distinctly." Here again, the weak sense of the expression is just a repudiation of formal foundationalism.

Throughout this book I have been arguing that the myth of the framework owes its plausibility entirely to invidious comparison with formal foundationalism. Those who hold the myth are constantly committing the fallacy of incomplete alternatives by trying to affirm the myth merely by denying formal foundationalism. In our discussion of tolerance we have seen the same process at work. The "intolerance" of formal foundationalism that results from its logical tendency to be over-sure of its own conclusions is attacked—and then the myth of the framework is affirmed as the tolerant alternative. But there is another form of foundationalism that does not suffer from the intolerance of formal foundationalism. This informal foundationalism makes possible the grounding of our convictions in favor of toleration and individual liberties in sources beyond convention. Thus grounded, our traditions of toleration seem far less threatened by the vagaries of the skeptic's arbitrary choice.

"Toleration" has been the ark of Western liberal thought. Its connection with skepticism and conventionalism, and now the myth of the framework, was and is an historical accident. In the next, brief chapter, I shall try to complete its recapture from the Philistines.

Chapter IX

THE UNTRUTHED GENERATION

In an article entitled "Nothing Matters,"[1] R. M. Hare argues, in effect, that nothing is to be gained by going beyond convention to find some further ground for morality. No such further ground can add anything to what convention alone provides:

> Think of one world into whose fabric values are objectively built; and think of another in which those values have been annihilated. And remember that in both worlds the people in them go on being concerned about the same things—there is no difference in the "subjective" concern which people have for things, only their "objective" value. Now I ask, "What is the difference between the states of affairs in these two worlds?" Can any answer be given except "None whatever"?[2]

Once again we have a case of storytelling to make a point, as if logical possibility were our only concern. I intend to show that Hare constructs this story by abstracting from all the elements in the debate that are unfavorable to "subjectivism" But first, please notice that there is at last one important area of agreement between Hare and myself. In the last chapter, I argued that skeptical conventionalism has no corner on the "toleration" market, that people who affirm that morality has a ground beyond convention are at least as likely to be tolerant as those who deny it. By saying there is no practical difference between these two ethical orientations,

---

[1]In R. M. Hare, *Applications of Moral Philosophy* (London: Oxford University Press, 1972) 42.

[2]Ibid.

Hare implicitly agrees that skeptical conventionalism is not, as such, *particularly* tolerant. Hare should also agree that toleration cannot be used as a special argument in favor of skeptical conventionalism, including its contemporary form, the myth of the framework.

The question from which Hare abstracts when he declares the two views identical is whether bare conventionalism is practically or even logically sustainable. It is the pairing of skepticism with conventionalism that raises the logical question. The pairing seems both inevitable and self-destructive. The skeptic, having repudiated all other grounds for morality, politics, and scientific knowledge, must turn to convention if he is to propose any intersubjective ground whatever for commonly held beliefs. But from the skeptic's own point of view, all that he repudiated in the first place was itself nothing but convention. It was, for example, merely a convention to say that there are grounds for belief other than convention. The skeptic aims his big guns at this and other conventions. But then suddenly, when he surely seems on the verge of destroying all that is necessary for common political and moral life, his guns fall silent. The conventions he arbitrarily decides to leave standing are then allowed to form the backbone of our moral and political life together. But what a weak backbone it is! The method by which it is left standing is an unnegotiated cease-fire in place. Nietzsche surely had all the logic of the argument on his side when he just went right on shooting, to leave nothing standing but individual creativity and no one brave enough to exercise it but the *Uebermensch.*

Even at this final outpost for the "subjective," however, we are left to wonder why the skeptical shooting has stopped. On what ground does Nietzsche praise *Uebermenschen?* Clearly not becase of convention. But then the only defense he has against the skeptical fusillade is a ground for value other than convention. Nietzsche, then, overcomes the self-destructive contradictions of skeptical conventionalism by giving up both skepticism and conventionalism. There appears to be no other way. But does he merely create for himself a value for the *Uebermensch?* Then he is merely proposing another unnegotiated cease-fire in place, sparing his own creation just as skeptical conventionalists spare some conventions rather than others, for no reason.[3]

---

[3]I will return to the discussion of existentialism in the final chapter.

Nor do appeals to coherence, holism, or pragmatism overcome the gargantuan arbitrariness. Pace Kant, people can be coherently tolerant or intolerant—it's only a matter of choice among the conventions. Holism, if it goes beyond the requirements of coherence, must stipulate a whole in terms of which it sets its standards. But such a whole must in turn be either a product of convention, of metaphysics,[4] or of individual choice. Metaphysics would require that the skeptic give up skepticism, whereas convention and individual choice contribute nothing to the mitigation of arbitrariness. Finally, pragmatism, if it is to go beyond coherence, must stipulate an end toward which it works, even if this end is defined merely as the result, whatever it may be, of a favored method. Once again such an end or method must rest on convention, metaphysics, or individual choice—and we have made no progress.

The reason for this recapitulation here of earlier arguments is to clear the road for the central claim of this chapter: skeptical conventionalism undermines the capacity of any society to pass on its traditions to the next generation. Hare claims that there is no practical difference between one group of people who express a set of cares and concerns based on what they take to be objective grounds and another group of people who express the very same set of cares and concerns for reasons of convention alone. But this begs the question whether people would have the same set of cares and concerns if they were based on convention alone. If I show concern for someone because it is the convention to do so, am I showing the same concern I would if his intrinsic worth inspires my support? As a ground for doing things, bare convention lacks cogency. It takes on the appearance of cogency to the extent that it hides itself as the ultimate ground and lets other grounds appear to operate. Thus, we might say that, indeed, I should help a fellow human being because of his intrinsic worth; but, of course, granting him this worth has no basis other than convention. This says no more than that I should help him because it is the convention to do so, though the bareness is scantily covered over. Vague references to "holism" and "pragmatism" are highly prized by the conventionalist to add further layers of clothing. Bare conventionalism's lack of cogency is nowhere more apparent than in

---

[4]Here I continue to use "metaphysics" in the broad sense described in Chapter 7: insight, based on observation, where the variables are too complex to be controlled for empirical (usually experimental) verification.

the problems it creates for trying to pass on traditions to the next generation. These problems will lead us to the heart of our discussion.

Learning a convention is a matter of learning what behavior is generally approved or disapproved within a group and acting accordingly to gain approval or at least to avoid disapproval. Almost everyone would agree that this form of learning is essential to the training of young children, so that they can begin as early as possible to exercise self-control, goal-direction, and respect for the rights of others. But at some point in a child's education, it becomes important to give rationales for behavior, rationales that go beyond concerns about approval and disapproval. This is less necessary, and perhaps even unnecessary, in societies that are extremely traditional, that is, societies without a tradition of inquiry in which questioning and skepticism play a central role. In such societies, there is virtually no counterweight to the control of tradition. Since very little winnowing of traditions takes place, rationales for conventional behavior go untested for long periods of time and can be left undeveloped without threatening the conventions themselves. Such traditionalism does not prevail in contemporary Western societies, however. We have a highly developed tradition of skeptical questioning that children soon drink in as part of their early conditioning. Thus activated, children begin at some point to expect explanations for how they are required to behave that go beyond simple approval and disapproval. Given the role that skeptical questioning plays in our culture, it is only reasonable that children be tendered such explanations to the extent that they are able to understand them.

What are we to say about these explanations children are given? Are they in turn merely conventions? Are they, in other words, things to be believed only because believing them will earn approval and avoid disapproval? But then they will satisfy the child only to the extent that he does not know this. When he finds out, he feels cheated and begins his skeptical questioning once again. The capacity of skeptical conventionalism to pass on a tradition depends upon its capacity to posit rationales sufficiently diverting and complex to ultimately hide the fact that everything rests on approval and disapproval in the end—and nothing more. This fact must be hidden because, once exposed, the practices that rest upon it are shaken to their roots by skeptical questioning. Once the child, by now perhaps a young adult, finally learns that there is no answer to his questions except "This is the way we do it," he doesn't really believe the tradition any more.[5] Only those who never make the full trip can believe any of the explanations offered along the way. The result is a generation that is radically untruthed and untraditioned. They can, of course, go on acting to earn approval and to avoid disapproval; but as the enlightenment that we are completely in the dark spreads, we are no longer able to approve or disapprove with conviction. Everything was made to depend upon custom, but custom cannot carry the burden without foundations of its own. It lies scattered and broken across the stygian sky.

To the extent that the young take the entire trip plotted for them by skeptical conventionalism, the result is what I call the "untruthed generation." This generation embodies the effects of the contradiction between: (1) being skeptical of everything as nothing more than convention, while (2) using convention as the only basis for conviction. The members of the untruthed generation know in their bones that they cannot have it both ways. They must either give up conviction or give up skepticism.

(1) Those who give up conviction are the ones who feel somewhat resentful when they discover that all they were told to believe is nothing but convention. They feel they have been subjected to manipulation and coercion. They fear ever to be convinced again because this would mean loss of freedom and autonomy.

Something very similar has happened in our sexual practices. In his book *Freedom and Destiny,* Rollo May describes a young woman who in her first counseling session stated that she was "entirely happy with her lover and did not want to have sex outside the relationship. But her lover had persuaded her that something was wrong if she could not go to bed with other men. The message behind her lover's concern was clear: *Is not an essential*

---

[5]The problem for the skeptical conventionalist is not the same as the one Socrates (*Republic,* bk. 3) tried to solve with his "noble lie." Socrates suggested that people be taught a myth about their origins and thereby be made more willing to accept the rigors of pure meritocracy. The myth was a lie only in that the events it described did not literally take place. Socrates' problem was to find a device to help the unphilosophical accept a system he regarded as truly and objectively wise and good. The "noble lie" was a *mythical* presentation of the truth Socrates was trying to inculcate, made understandable and, he hoped, palatable to the masses. Socrates expresses clearly the conviction that in important matters, people cannot be motivated by appeals to convention alone. They require the "objective grounds" the noble lie tried mythically to supply, and which the philosopher could grasp more directly.

part of being free the freedom to have sexual intercourse with whomever one wants, whenever one is so inclined?"[6] Those who see sexual fidelity as a matter of convention, especially if they also believe they have been manipulated and controlled by others in the past, experience exclusive sexual commitment as a form of oppression—a giving in to the pressures of convention and a failure in the courage to be free. It is commonplace among marriage counselors to find men and women who are happy with their marriage partners but nevertheless need to fool around on the side to reassure themselves constantly that they are "still the boss," still in charge of their own lives and not controlled by someone else. Commitment and even emotional intimacy itself are feared and resisted in the name of freedom.

The experience of this "unloved generation" parallels that of the "untruthed generation" and has similar causes. For the "untruthed," conviction poses the same threat that commitment and intimacy pose for the "unloved"—the threat of being manipulated and controlled by others for their own purposes. But a life empty of conviction, like a life empty of emotional intimacy, seems a high price to pay for freedom. Unless one thought of conviction as nothing more than slavery to convention, one would probably not think such a life free at all.

(2) Those who give up skepticism rather than conviction are those who feel somewhat bereaved when they hear that all they have believed is nothing but convention. They remember their beliefs with nostalgia rather than with resentment—recalling the comfort, direction, inspiration, and strength that came from them. Faced with a choice between what seems to them the wasteland of skepticism and the attraction of belief, they finally choose the latter. But they realize they cannot do so and continue the conventions of skepticism. Unplugging critical thought, they may join a community of *dogmatic* convictions under an authoritarian leader—a cult group, a cadre of revolutionaries, or a fundamentalist branch of a mainline religion. Here we have the leap of faith with a vengeance. For such people it is skepticism and critical thinking that are the main threat, instruments of the devil, perhaps, to take away their faith. It is hard for the rest of us, who are part of the skeptical culture, to understand these cultists; but they are the products of that same skeptical culture, trying to resolve

[6]Rollo May, *Freedom and Destiny* (New York: Norton, 1981).

the unbearable contradictions of skeptical conventionalism. They find fideism more acceptable than the alternatives they seem faced with.

The two classes of the "untruthed generation" are, as one might expect, sometimes combined in a single person who has both resentment and nostalgia for belief, at times feeling one more than the other but never eliminating either. There are also many additional factors that combine with the choice of (1) or (2). It is possible that some people opt for (1) or (2) for emotional or psychological reasons not connected with epistemology. I would conjecture that this is rare, however; our culture's epistemological uneasiness has become pervasive and shows itself in many, apparently unrelated, permutations of panic.

Here's what I hope this exploration of the contradictions of skeptical conventionalism has made clear: if we are to maintain the progressive nature of our intellectual culture, with its skeptical/critical components, we must recognize a basis for conviction other than convention. When Richard Rorty invites us into an intellectual space where there are no more arguments and no more views, he is inviting us to understand the meaning of the myth of the framework. When skepticism no longer has anything to work against, what is the point of arguing? When our beliefs are nothing more than products of conditioning and convention, they are no longer views of anything and therefore not views at all. Two chapters ago, after what seemed at the time to be crunching arguments against the myth, I delayed final judgment in order to investigate the claim made on behalf of the myth that it fosters toleration. Investigation showed this claim to be the result of historical accident and largely an illusion. I then pressed the argument further and displayed the problems the myth (as a variety of skeptical conventionalism) creates for passing on culture and tradition to the next generation. I conclude that the self-contradictions of the myth do not serve well the needs of a progressive society.

By now the reader is able to anticipate easily the remedy I would offer for the problem caused by the myth. Informal foundationalism exemplifies the combination of realism and skepticism that a progressive society requires. I did not make this point earlier in the book because I did not want it to appear that my argument is primarily a pragmatic one. This would have been to seem to accept the assumptions of the myth of the framework even while arguing against it. Vague appeals to "pragmatism" have, after all, been frequently used to assure us that, despite being empty of content, the myth of the framework can offer us something. In the next chapter I will suggest that pragmatism has a natural connection with realism, and their separation is an academic aberration with no other very specific source than the general skepticism of the age.

Chapter X

ON BEING A PRAGMATIST

What is the difference between a realist and a pragmatist? In popular usage the connotations are similar: both are thought to have their feet on the ground, to show a strong concern for the facts, to reject the impractical or visionary, and to have a high regard for the methods of science. It is only when we see the realist and the pragmatist as members of rival academic schools that we become aware of basic differences. The realist, at least the one this book is about, bases his predilection for observation and scientific method upon a realistic epistemology. He remains convinced, for reasons we have been discussing, that observation gives us unique access to things as they are; and all theory, whether verifiable or not, starts from an effort to explain the observable. Occasionally a theory achieves such a high degree of success that we say it is not only confirmed but true—true in just the way that observation statements can be true. By means of true theories and observation statements—and the concepts they express—we come to a partial knowledge of things as they are in themselves, that is, as they are independent of our observations and thoughts of them or statements about them.

The pragmatist, on the other hand, shares the Kantian problematic. Pragmatism developed in the United States during a time when idealism was the dominant philosophical fashion. Reacting to idealism, Peirce, James, and Dewey wanted to debunk what they saw as the visionary excesses of idealist metaphysics. They did this by reemphasizing the importance of experience and science, but their reasons for this emphasis were quite different from those of the realist. When I say they shared "the Kantian problematic," I mean they shared with Kant the assumption that any foundation for knowledge in awareness of things-themselves was untenable. It is not hard to understand why they shared Kant's mistake in this. The forms of realism familiar to them would have been couched in terms of correspondence theory, representationalism, and formal foundationalism. Peirce, James, and Dewey were particularly opposed to correspondence theory and representationalism. They vigorously attacked the image theory of thought with which "ideas" had been linked by Descartes, Locke, Berkeley, Hume, and others. Trying to verify our ideas without using ideas was hopeless, and the futility led to skepticism. To avoid skepticism, the pragmatists gave up the goal of "correspondence," which was impossible to achieve, given the representationalist starting point. Dewey's "instrumentalism" defined ideas as tools for directing our activities rather than as images. This changed understanding of the fundamental nature of thought he took to be the essence of pragmatism.

But we are moving too quickly. Why did the pragmatists view idealism with alarm? Why did they prefer to prune back its visionary excesses by appeal to experience and scientific method? Remember the pragmatists are not realists. They are not claiming that observation offers unique access to the real and for that reason that metaphysical theories which undermine or contradict ordinary perceptual knowledge are to be rejected. They are not foundationalists, they are holists. Peirce and Dewey are strong advocates of scientific method because it is the method that has the greatest success spawning general agreement concerning its results. It is this general agreement or harmony that the pragmatists set before us as the ethical and aesthetic goal of all human activity. If we ask of pragmatism, "Pragmatic to what end?" or of instrumentalism, "Instrumental to what end?"—the answer is "general harmony." The closer we stay to experience and scientific method, the more likely we are to agree with one another and to avoid endless and fruitless discussions that can produce no such agreement. Pragmatism, as the name implies, is a teleological system, and the goal it sets before us is the harmony of a unified whole.

Dewey describes scientific inquiry in the appropriate holist terms. "Primary experience" gives rise to conflicts and inconsistencies. These spur one to exercise "secondary thinking" in order to resolve the uneasy, problematic situation. Inquiry "is the controlled or directed transformation of an indeterminate situation into one that is so determinate in its constituent distinctions and relations as to convert the elements of the original situation into a unified whole."[1] Ideas produced along the way of inquiry are to be treated as hypotheses to be tested experimentally. When the results of these testing procedures are favorable, the inquirer can eventually achieve an experience of "satisfaction," and the ideas that give satisfaction by resolving the initiating problematic are called "knowledge."[2] Knowledge terminates inquiry, just as doubt begins it. We shall see that, for Dewey, the movement to more and more inclusive states of harmonious satisfaction characterizes scientific method, the life of the intelligent human being, and the progress of a democratic society.

Peirce uses different terminology to say, in general, the same thing. For Peirce, the common desire for the sort of harmony that science affords is called the "social impulse."[3] Peirce's well-known "end of inquiry," his standard of truth, is but the idealized harmony of opinion that eventuates when there are no problems left for science to solve. For some reason, and Peirce says nothing to explain it, people are readier to agree upon ideas from observation and science than on ideas from other sources. Therefore, once we are ruled by an ethical concern for universal satisfaction and harmony, we should emphasize science and set aside brands of inquiry that breed disagreement and disharmony of the sort that is never resolved.

This last point explains why Dewey and Peirce reject idealistic metaphysics while at the same time accepting what we might call the idealist ethics and aesthetics of harmony. Idealist metaphysics is just the sort of thing that people do not agree on. Therefore, in the name of general harmony and satisfaction, this metaphysics was to be eschewed in favor of science, whose methods are more generally satisfying and more generally accepted.

Once we understand that the desire for general harmony is the ethical engine that powers Peirce's and Dewey's allegiance to sci-

---

[1]John Dewey, *Logic: The Theory of Inquiry* (New York: H. Holt, 1938) 104-105.

[2]Ibid., 8.

[3]C. S. Peirce, *Collected Papers*, 8 vols., Anthony Burks, Charles Hartshorne, and Paul Weiss, eds. (Cambridge: Harvard University Press, 1931-1958) 5:381.

ence, we can penetrate one famous disagreement they had with William James. All three agree that "true idea" means "useful idea." But useful for what purposes? As we have seen, Peirce and Dewey make "useful for general harmony" their dominant priority and acknowledge science as its most fit instrument. James does not see things the same way. James believed an idea could be "true" (that is, useful) to an individual as well as to general society. If a particular individual found an idea useful in conducting his life in a positive way, then that idea is true for him. On just such grounds, James argued for belief in God and in an afterlife,[4] noting the satisfaction (support, meaning) such ideas give.

Peirce and Dewey were appalled that such ideas be put on a par with the ideas of science. But they should not be mistaken for hard positivists next to James's soft existentialism. No positivist could accept Pierce's and Dewey's grounding of science in ethics and aesthetics any more than he could accept James's belief in the afterlife. All three pragmatists grounded truth in its service to the ethical goal of harmony and satisfaction. James is just more individualistic about it. Peirce and Dewey insist upon the hegemony of science because the harmony they idealize is the widest possible social harmony. Arguments for God's existence or for an afterlife do not produce the degree of general agreement that science does. For the sake of wide social harmony, they are to be set aside. James, on the other hand, emphasizes that individual harmony is something of great value also. Those who have experienced the advantages of belief in God and afterlife have discovered a truth that is not falsified by the mere fact that many others may never discover it. Too bad for them.

As I have already said, we will badly misunderstand this difference between James and his fellow pragmatists if we see him as a dreamer and them as positivists. The difference was nothing but a matter of ethical taste: the weighting of social versus individual satisfactions. The nature of the disagreement, once understood, exposes the soft underbelly of pragmatism. As a philosophical system, pragmatism historically stood foursquare upon the exclusive and self-evident moral goodness of the satisfactions derived from greater and greater harmony. This basis is soft because it is malleable to so many very different points of view.

---

[4]William James, *Pragmatism* (Indianapolis: Hackett, 1981) bk. 8.

Peirce and Dewey saw these harmonies primarily in terms of society as a whole. Dewey constructed a liberal theory of government upon his social harmony base. He thought free-ranging individual intelligence and democratic institutions would provide the best hope for solving problems and achieving harmony through experimentation. Marx, Lenin, Hitler, and Mussolini also espoused the general aim of ultimate harmony but were often willing to embrace less than liberal means to achieve it. Dewey can argue that their means do not work as well as his own do, but this point will be hard to make out through the pragmatist cloud. Ultimate harmonies can, after all, be defined variously (classless society, the Super State, and so forth.) and the means to them specified accordingly (class warfare, suppression of minorities, and so forth.). From the viewpoint of fascist and communist harmonies, Dewey's praise of democratic institutions appears effete.

Ultimate harmonies are never verifiable experimentally, and as George Sorel and many other revolutionaries have told us, short-term harmony, by fostering illusionary complacency, may actually get in the way of the bigger and better harmonies that lie on the other side of turmoil. Harmony itself becomes a problem to be dealt with when we recognize it as a sop against bigger progress. How, on pragmatist grounds, does one resolve the disagreement between those who regard the harmonies produced by democracy as confirmation of democratic ideology and those who regard them as veneer and obstruction? The quandary results from trying to hang so much, indeed everything, upon a vague, free-floating, and general value like "harmony." No one is against harmony, but it is such a shifting foundation for the structures Dewey tries to build upon it.

Let's examine one of these most cherished structures in more detail: the place, the value, and role of science itself. James claims that "God exists" and "There is an afterlife" are true because believing them has very useful and positive effects upon one's life. Peirce and Dewey do not agree that such happy consequences render these statements true. Most people would surely agree with Peirce and Dewey on this point, whether they believe these statements true on other grounds or not. But the fact that we are inclined to side with Peirce and Dewey should not blind us to the following: from a pragmatist point of view, Peirce and Dewey do not have a strong case against James. They can chide him for not appreciating enough the "social impulse" and the unique mandate it gives to science. They can expostulate when James says some things that are not authorized by science. But James can reply that their sense of harmony is too narrow and fails to recognize the importance of the individual's struggle for satisfactory meaning in his own life. When told that many will not accept the harmony-inducing religious beliefs that James says are true, he can simply express sincere sympathy for the agnostics of the world and wish them better luck in the future. Which side has the advantages in this debate? If we judge on pragmatic grounds alone, I think we surely must say: neither. As a dispute among pragmatists, it is just a matter of one's taste for harmonies, which kind one prefers. Peirce's and Dewey's adherence to *sola scientia* is strongly stated; but, as James has shown, it is weakly based. Once we equate the truth of an idea with the harmony and satisfaction the idea brings to our experience, the idea of heavenly bliss looks truer than any scientific theory likely to be devised. Granted it cannot be arrived at scientifically, among pragmatists exclusive obsession with science is just one sectarian piety. James offers another.

I believe that honest self-examination will reveal that the reason most of us are uneasy about James's argument for the existence of God is that, despite heavy bombardment, our realist spontaneity has yet not been entirely snuffed out. It is this same spontaneity that can make us uneasy about pragmatism in general when we realize it lacks the resources to deal with James's challenge. To the realist, James's mistake is as plain as day. Truth is not just a matter of felicitous coherence among our ideas and actions. For the realist, a statement is true if it fits reality; and reality is that which exists and is what it is independently of what anyone thinks, feels, desires, or wishes. To come to know that God exists, one must have evidence that God is real in this sense. It is not enough to have evidence that believing God exists will pay off in a more positive and fruitful life. But if most of us are at least residual realists, we may nevertheless feel uneasy about indulging our realist spontaneity in this way. Hasn't realism been shown untenable by attacks on correspondence theory and foundationalism?It is the entire point of this book to show that it has not. Rather, the strong realist alternative may free us to honestly admit our uneasiness about pragmatism sans realism.

Early critics of James's and Dewey's respective notions of truth were satisfied to show how they contradicted ordinary usage. Bertrand Russell, it is true, mounted a criticism that can be used against all forms of ethical consequentialism and utilitarianism.

He observed that it was impossible to determine whether the net outcome of holding a belief will be—or even has been—positive or negative. The consequences are so entwined with those of entirely different causes. He concluded that the pragmatist criterion of truth, harmonious consequences, was impractical because the net consequences were incalculable. He proposed realist procedures as the practical alternative.[5] Later in this chapter I shall follow a related, but more general, line to argue that realism is more practical than pragmatism, thus defeating pragmatism on its own ground. For now, however, I want to survey another sort of argument Russell used against James's notion of truth and that Carnap and Moore used against Dewey's notion of truth.

Russell observed that if James's notion of truth were correct, then the sentences "It is true that other people exist" and "It is useful to believe other people exist" would have the same meaning and express the same proposition. Russell appeals to ordinary usage to show that they do not. He concludes that James's notion of truth is, at best, woefully inadequate.

Carnap similarly attacks Dewey's notion that an idea becomes true only when it is confirmed by an investigator. He shows that ordinary usage distinguishes between "is true" and "is confirmed."[6] It contradicts ordinary usage to say that "The earth is spherical" became true only when evidence proved that it was, and that it was not true before then. Carnap goes on to observe that Dewey's notion of truth as confirmation contradicts the law of excluded middle. According to Dewey, the statement "Either the earth is flat or it is not flat" was not, prior to confirmation one way or the other, true. It was not true because neither of the disjuncts *can* be true until it (either disjunct) is confirmed. If neither disjunct is true, then their disjunction is not true. "P or not P" is no longer a necessary truth.

G. E. Moore added the following criticism, once again based upon ordinary usage. There is only one sense in which we may make a belief true: when we actually bring about that which the belief stipulates. I can make true my belief that I will rise at seven tomorrow by actually rising at seven tomorrow. But I do not make

---

[5]Bertrand Russell, "Pragmatism" and "William James' Conception of Truth," in his *Philosophical Essays* (New York: Norton, 1910).

[6]Rudolf Carnap, "Truth and Confirmation," in H. Feigel and W. Sellars, eds., *Readings in Philosophical Analysis* (New York: Appleton-Century-Crofts, 1949).

a belief true by inquiry into its truth. Inquiry does not make something true; it only makes that which is true *known.*[7]

We will think highly of these ordinary language criticisms of pragmatism by Russell, Carnap, and Moore, if we think ordinary language is the court of last appeal in such matters. Dewey, for one, certainly did not believe it was. He was out to reform logic, language, and culture in general. Russell, Moore and Carnap wanted badly to be realists, after all, and they found ordinary usage congenial to their philosophical predispositions. But the realism of Russell, Moore, and Carnap was on its way to collapse, as Dewey may or may not have sensed. The realism of ordinary usage and ordinary logic did not serve the more ultimate synthesis Dewey was trying to bring about. This early-twentieth-century version of the debate between realists and pragmatists can be construed as another example of conflict between two harmonies. Russell, Carnap, and Moore can be seen as advocates of the more immediate harmonies of ordinary usage—they are inclined to rule out discordant notions like the pragmatist view of truth. Dewey is, in this instance, the prophet of greater and more distant harmonies that require the overthrow of ordinary usage. It is harmony versus harmony again, synthesis versus synthesis, the old Hegelian dilemma. It seems that appeals to ordinary usage do not press the discussion deeply enough to be decisive.

The pragmatists can, after all, go far to placate the sensibilities of common sense. While it is true that only the commodious results of inquiry render an idea true, once an idea is rendered true by its predictive or other success, we can in retrospect speak of it as having been true all along, that is, as having been all along an idea that could bring inquiry to a further advance in synthesis. The retrospective viewpoint was the genius of Peirce's talk of "the end of inquiry" as the standard of truth. From the vantage point of the end of inquiry, all possible statements can be seen retrospectively as more or less true or false. This way of putting the matter re-explains ordinary usage, but does not replace it. It also shows how the law of excluded middle can continue to be applied. Every statement can be seen as retrospectively true or false from the viewpoint of some mythical future time when evidence will finally decide it. Pragmatists have reason to believe they have ad-

---

[7] G. E. Moore, "William James' Pragmatism," in his *Philosophical Studies* (New York: Harcourt, Brace, 1922).

equately responded to the ordinary language attack. They advocate changes in ordinary usage, but are careful to displace it as little as possible.

PRAGMATIST ETHICS

Given the central position of ethical considerations in the pragmatist system, it is impossible to discuss the pragmatist theory of truth or of knowledge without discussing ethics as well. I have already mentioned Russell's misgivings about the incalculable nature of the pragmatist standard of truth. I have also observed that a telos like "ultimate harmony" is itself so indeterminate as to foster a sense of helpless confusion when used to adjudicate among contradictory political and other claims. Clearly, a full-blown discussion of ethics would be out of place in a book on epistemology. The following remarks about pragmatist ethics seem unavoidable, however; as much as possible they shall be kept in close proximity to the main concerns of the present work.

We have already discussed to some extent John Dewey's notion of the ethically good as "ultimate harmony." Such harmony is for him the moral telos of all human activity. If general harmony or satisfaction is the *form* of the good for Dewey, then impulse is its *matter*. For him the morally good is the set of consequences capable of satisfying human impulses better than any available alternative set. In *Democracy and Education*[8] he describes education as the formation of the child's inchoate energies so that the child acts in ways maximally satisfying to both its own and others' impulses. This is not a mere indoctrination with societal conventions. The most important vehicle for the channeling of impulse, Dewey claimed, is intelligence. When impulses are not adequately satisfied, intelligence comes into play to solve the problem. Intelligence may find that certain conventions are the source of the problem and need to be revised. Thus education included for Dewey two objectives: (1) indoctrination with the acquired wisdom of a particular culture; (2) development of intelligence to revise the conventions of the culture when they no longer serve well the goal of general satisfaction.

This appeal to impulse organization as the ground of morality has a long pedigree, prominently including Hobbes and Freud. There can be no doubt that in a child's moral development some-

---

[8]John Dewey, *Democracy and Education* (New York: MacMillan, 1916).

thing like impulse organization does take place. The child learns the acceptable ways to express emotions and desires. Granted all this, however, the explanation of moral principles and moral concerns in terms of impulse organization seems an explanation *clarius per obscurius.* It seems more obvious that slandering, defrauding, or damaging the health of another are immoral than that they are inefficient ways for individuals in society to discharge their basic impulses. Dewey can answer that the macro-level is more obvious only because we have been indoctrinated by the mores of a culture. Perhaps. But assuming so is only to beg the question. When would we ever need to trace our morality to the wilderness of basic impulses to decide how to discharge them with maximum efficiency? I should say we never would; and if we ever did, we would find the attempt quite hopeless.

What then is the point of talking of impulse organization as if it explained something? Such talk, it seems, serves two theoretical purposes: (1) It reduces the evaluative to the mechanical, showing how evaluative terms can be eliminated at the most basic level of explanation. In other words, it serves the general project of reductive or eliminative materialism. But this general project has already been decisively stopped at another point—the many ingenious attempts to reduce or eliminate the mental in favor of the micro-physical have failed. I argued earlier that our reductionist obsessions are the product of a love affair with mathematics, a fascination with the simplicities of calculus. If my earlier arguments were successful, and if we use them to break the hold of our calculational infatuation, we will not find cogent this first reason for reducing the moral to impulse organization.

(2) Talk of impulse organization will give us a sufficiently fluid view of human nature to allow for different moral principles and moral concerns in different cultures and circumstances. Such reasoning is clearly what motivated Dewey. He was leery of what he regarded as too rigid moralities. It was this concern that led Dewey to strongly deny the existence of a *summum bonum* or ultimate good.

At first this denial by Dewey may seem curious, since his own ethics can be so exhaustively described in terms of "ultimate harmony" or "maximally efficient discharge of impulse." Are not such notions the sort that are meant by a *summum bonum?* Dewey did not think so, but he misunderstood the classical discussion of the *summum bonum.* He apparently thought it was about some single, univocal property of all good actions or experiences. Such a *summum bonum,* he rightly thought, would result in a damagingly inflexible view of human nature and morality. Aristotle's *eudaimonia,* more recently rendered by Abraham Maslow's "self-actualization," is a classical statement of a *summum bonum* that does not suffer the univocal inflexibility Dewey feared.

Granted the need for flexibility from culture to culture and from circumstance to circumstance, the appeal to impulse organization is nevertheless dysfunctional. Appeal to it is never needed to explain differences in mores from culture to culture. Suppose we are comparing the dietary laws of two cultures. We can explain how in each culture these laws serve concerns for health, hygiene, religious purity, and so forth. At no point is it necessary to find common grounds for comparison by reduction to impulse. Nothing more than analysis in terms of generally understandable values is required to give us the flexibility needed to compare cultures and circumstances efficiently and accurately. Unless we are closet reductionists to begin with, Dewey's concern for cultural flexibility will not inspire us to adopt his impulse analysis of morality. Generally understood values such as survival, health, religious concern, aesthetic appreciation, rearing the next generation, and so forth, give us all we need for cross-cultural analysis.[9]

So far I have discussed problems with the twin ethical bases of Dewey's philosophical orientation, "ultimate harmony" and "impulse organization." My complaint has been that neither is useful. "Ultimate harmony" is not useful becase it is too vague to help us decide among competing theories, and, more specifically, that it is too vague to establish Dewey's ideas about the hegemony of science and of democracy. "Impulse organization" is not useful because it is never needed as common ground in cross-cultural analysis of values; and as part of reductive materialism, it participates in a strategy that is a failure as a whole.

---

[9]I am inclined to go further than this and to claim that such general values are basic to our moral thinking and serve as its foundations. Elaboration and defense of *this* wonderful thesis would take more space than is appropriate here, but the way has already been shown by such recent works as Mortimer Adler, *Six Great Ideas* (New York: Macmillan, 1981); Germain Grisez (with R. Shaw), *Beyond the New Morality* (Notre Dame: Notre Dame University Press, 1974); William Galston, *Justice and the Human Good* (Chicago: University of Chicago Press, 1980); and especially John Finnis, *Natural Law and Natural Rights* (Oxford: Oxford University Press, 1980).

Before leaving this discussion of pragmatist ethics, I would like to comment upon two slogans that have been part of the pragmatist call for reform of philosophical language: (1) there is no distinction between means and ends; (2) there is no distinction between theory and practice. These slogans were meant to complete the task of overcoming the dualisms of traditional philosophy. I have already had much to say about the importance of overcoming soul/body, appearance/reality, and fact/value dualisms. Dewey attacks these dualisms too, but he goes on to find further hobgoblins in the means/end and theory/practice distinctions. Here I believe he was being carried away by an excessive passion for seamless holism.

(1) The means/end distinction, Dewey rightly observed, presupposes a distinction between intrinsic and instrumental goods, a distinction whose validity Dewey denies. Means and ends are functionally interactive,[10] says Dewey—there are no ends that are intrinsic goods. Dewey attempts to show this by pointing out that a reasonable man who finds his ends impossible to attain will revise them to better fit a realistic assessment of the means available.[11] Apparently Dewey thinks this shows that means rule ends as much as ends rule means, which is apparently what he means by saying that they are functionally interactive.

Dewey is surely right about what the reasonable person, in such a case, would do. It is not clear, however, that the example shows that means rule ends as much as ends rule means. The *availability* of means rules the *possibility* of ends, but it does not rule their *desirability* or *intrinsic goodness.* In other words, the fact that means are not available to pursue a particular end does not show that it is not an intrinsically good end. An example will make this clear. Suppose we are on a battlefield during the American Civil War. A soldier has a serious leg wound. I would say that restoration of the soldier to full health and physical integrity would be an intrinsically good end. This would include saving the leg. Suppose the means are not available (as they would be in an American hospital in the late twentieth century) to save the leg. Instead, in order to save the soldier's life, the leg must be ampu-

---

[10]John Dewey, *Quest for Certainty* (London: G. Allen and Unwin, 1930) 38-39.

[11]John Dewey, *Human Nature and Conduct* (New York: Modern Library, 1930) ch. 6.

tated. Dewey is right: the reasonable course, under the circumstances, is to amputate the leg. But how does this prove that restoration to full health was not an intrinsic good? Rather, in this case, the choice of the means (amputation) was ruled by the closest approximation to this good possible. (No one suggests that the soldier should be shot through the head or left completely untreated when care is available). The doctrine that there are intrinsic goods does not imply that these goods are always realizable, or even that they are always to be concretely chosen, all things considered, when they are realizable. If it did imply this, it would indeed be an excessively rigid moral doctrine. But it is only against this excessive doctrine that Dewey's objection works. It does not show that goods like full health are not intrinsic goods. Since Dewey's attack on intrinsic goods fails, his corollary against the means/end distinction also fails.

Once we correct Dewey's understanding of "intrinsic good," we can see that "ultimate harmony" is, in his own ethics, an intrinsic good. For Dewey, harmony is instrumental only toward further harmony. Harmony is always the goal of moral concern. It is one means among many, but it is the preeminent end.

(2) It is not hard to grasp why Dewey was opposed to the theory/practice distinction. He denies that theoretical or intellectual understanding is an intrinsic good or end in itself. Such understanding is, for Dewey, always at the service of "ultimate harmony;" its function is to enable us to discharge our impulses in maximally satisfactory ways by solving the problems that impede us. Theory is thus subsumed under practice. All the premises for Dewey's attack upon the theory/practice distinction have been attacked above: the notions (1) that ultimate harmony is the goal of all human activity, (2) that there are no intrinsic goods or ends in themselves, (3) that ethics can be usefully grounded upon the organization of impulse. Dewey is at least right to this extent, however: theoretical activity can be seen as good from an ethical point of view every bit as much as ethical theory can be seen as true from a theoretical point of view. To this extent the two are reciprocally related. But the real issue is whether intellectual activity can be seen as good in itself or whether it must be seen, as Dewey claims, *only* as instrumental toward some other good, namely, ultimate harmony or satisfaction.

But even on Dewey's own terms, this case is far from clear. Understanding is, after all, one sort of harmony, one sort of problem resolution. Theoretical problems look toward theoretical solutions. And surely ultimate harmony as an ideal must be construed as in part constituted by theoretical and contemplative harmony. Dewey himself strongly emphasizes the importance of the aesthetic consummations that he identifies with these achieved states of intellectual harmony. But then this good of intellectual harmony, which constitutes in part the ultimate end and the intrinsic good, participates, to that extent, in being itself ultimate end and intrinsic good. It is hard to imagine what more a defender of the theory/practice distinction would want. Intellectual harmony is not only good, it is good in itself. It is not, of course, all that is good; but a complete vision of goodness (as ultimate harmony or whatever) must, even for Dewey, include it as a constituent part. It is, therefore, not merely instrumental to the achievement of the ultimate good. But it was by showing theoretical knowledge to be merely instrumental that Dewey tried to blur the theory/practice distinction. Since theoretical knowledge is an intrinsic good, the theory/practice distinction stands.

Dewey could reply that "ultimate harmony" is not likely ever to be achieved and that therefore no theoretical knowledge we experience will ever participate in ultimate harmony—it will be just a step upon the way. It follows that no theoretical knowledge we will ever experience will be an intrinsic good, only an instrumental good. But the point of mentioning "ultimate harmony" was not to suggest that it would ever happen, nor does the thesis that theoretical knowledge is an intrinsic good require that the day of ultimate harmony ever arrive—any more than Peirce's "end of inquiry" will ever arrive. The point, rather, is the following. To show that theoretical knowledge is not an *intrinsic* good, one must show it is in the service of *some other* good. What the above argument shows is that a complete description of any such further good would include the consummatory harmony of theoretical knowledge, again and again ad infinitum. Theoretical knowledge is always included as part of the comprehensive further end; it is therefore, from such a perspective, never just a means but also an end. This is all we need to call it an "intrinsic good:" the fact that it is not just an instrumental good.

PRAGMATIC REALISM

Earlier in the chapter, I promised I would ring down the curtain on this discussion of pragmatism by showing that it is less useful, less satisfying, than the realism of informal foundationalism. This was a promise to defeat pragmatism on its own ground. Let's see if I can deliver on that promise.

The first point to be made is both an assertion and a challenge: there is nothing that pragmatism explains that informal foundationalism cannot explain equally well, if not better. Predictive and experimental success function strongly in the realist philosophy of science as they do for the pragmatist. Pragmatist ethics tends to depend on not very useful notions like "ultimate harmony" and "impulse organization." The realist can easily do as well—it seems to me much better—by emphasizing more intermediate notions of good: survival, health, knowledge, and so forth. Nothing more than these is needed for cross-cultural comparison.

On the other hand, informal foundationalism explains something that pragmatism does not explain. Dewey and Peirce emphasize the value of observation and scientific method because they serve as a basis for more unanimous opinions about things and thus promote social harmony. But Dewey and Peirce leave one very interesting question unanswered, and even unasked: why is it that people agree so much more easily about observations than they do about metaphysics, religion, or political ideology? Why this compulsion to agree about observations? Pragmatists have given up on this question. In their view, it was this question whose answers led to the picture theory of ideas and the general skepticism that followed from it. The pragmatists wanted nothing to do with this kind of skepticism. Their revulsion was understandable. But are we doomed to representationalism and skepticism if we try to answer the question, "Whence the compulsion of perception?"

By understanding observation as a unique access to things themselves, informal foundationalism offers an answer to this question that avoids the pitfalls the pragmatists feared. It serves up no picture theory of ideas and is unskeptical. It has greater explanatory power than pragmatism because it answers a question that made cowards of the pragmatists. Given its greater explanatory power, the only pragmatist reason we could have for rejecting it would be that it is in some way incoherent. A major thesis of this book has been that arguments that show realism to be incoherent work well against other forms of realism, but do not work at all against informal foundationalism. If this thesis is correct, then, even on pragmatist grounds, informal foundationalism should be preferred to pragmatism. Once the pragmatist embraces informal foundationalism with its greater explanatory power, he has become a realist. The irony is that he will also be a better pragmatist than ever.

The separation of pragmatism from realism was an academic aberration, a notion far from the popular view of the connection between the two orientations. In this case the popular view was right; the academic view created many problems that have already taken us very long to unravel.

Chapter XI

REALISM AND ARTISTIC FREEDOM

In my earlier chapters I have frequently made the point that the myth of the framework owes much of its attractiveness to the perception that is uniquely suited to dissolve troubling philosophical problems and to promote political toleration. To these apparent advantages of the myth may be added a third: its openness to artistic innovation.

It is clear that the myth would be a friend of freedom in the arts. According to the myth, a new art form needs for its legitimacy only to be locatable within some framework of interpretation, understanding, and aesthetic appreciation. This standard would seem to place no troublesome a priori limits upon the direction of artistic development. It simply allows a new art form and its framework to arise more or less together and to take their place among the explored possibilities of aesthetic projection and involvement.

By contrast, there has been a stricter tradition among "realist" philosophies. Plato, for example, regarded art as essentially imitative. The low status of art was then derived from the metaphysical principle, "That which imitates is less than that which is imitated." This low status meant that art and its appreciation were not self-justifying. Rather, art was justified by its effects. Plato himself applied a moral standard: art could be justified only if it encouraged virtue and discouraged vice. Joshua Reynolds, whose *Discourses on Art* insists unequivocally that art must always be more than mere imitation, nevertheless envisions this "more" exclusively in terms of an idealization of the real—whether in heroic painting or in flattering portraiture. Such criteria of artistic legitimacy would seem to rule out much that has passed for great art. Arthur Danto offers us a contemporary notion of art as imitation:

> That something is an imitation does not require that there is something of which it is an imitation: "i is an o-imitation" can be true though the world be o-less. All that is required is that from i we should be able to recognize o, if o's exist and i is a good o-imitation.[1]

This allows for pictures of elves and gremlins to be "imitations" though elves and gremlins do not exist. But such imitations would not include artistic configurations that stand much more "on their own," that is, that are not intended by the artist to denote anything real or imaginatively possible.[2]

A realist epistemology does not, however, imply a limitation to the "artistic realism" just described. What I wish to propose here is a rapprochement between epistemological realism and artistic open-mindedness. For the sort of realism I wish to defend, the study of knowledge and the study of art go in opposite directions. Knowledge is of that which already exists. Art is the making of something new. Now, one can make something new for various reasons. A common reason is so that the new thing may be used for some further purpose, as a tool. The new things that interest us here are not tools, however, but art objects, things made for the sake of the aesthetic satisfaction of creating and beholding them. An art object has its own integrity and completeness. It is not primarily a tool for making present things that are themselves absent, nor is it primarily a tool for moral betterment. An art object is meant to be appreciated on its own aesthetic merits, and its success is measured in terms of this appreciation.

But artistic creation is not creation *ex nihilo,* nor is aesthetic appreciation the act of a *tabula rasa.* Both art and the appreciation of art require multiple connections with the world. There are

---

[1]Arthur C. Danto, *The Transfiguration of the Commonplace* (Cambridge: Harvard University Press, 1981) 160.

[2]Danto would seem to agree with this point when he observes that "imitational structures" are too "parochial" to capture the whole of "artistic representation." Ibid., 82. Apparently Danto means by "*re*presentation" what could be better expressed as "presentation"; the latter expression avoids suggesting "duplication," which would carry us back to "imitation."

many media of such connections: other art works, religion, philosophy, acculturation, tradition, and one's own thoughtful, purposeful, emotional living—a loose and abbreviated list. Not only does the artist make use of paint, clay, sound, color, shape, rhythm, and so forth. Even the new forms he works into these materials are, often untraceably, connected with earlier experiences, ideas, emotions, insights, and influences. Art historians and critics help us to understand these multiple connections and by doing so help beholders of art to connect more richly their own experiences and ideas with an art work and to enhance their aesthetic appreciation of it. But a work of art must stand first on its own two feet as an object of aesthetic appreciation. The development of one's capacity for artistic understanding takes place primarily in the presence of art works, not from discussions of or lectures about art.

George Santayana spoke of the "expressiveness" of a work of art.[3] By this he meant the work's capacity to evoke conscious and unconscious associations that help constitute the experience of the art work as a meaningful and beautiful[4] integrated whole. The domain of art is entered from other domains of experience by both artist and beholder; and when the aesthetic moment is past, each returns to those other domains, carrying his multiple associations with him. The artistic domain flows creatively out of and into the other domains of life.

Notice that I am not attempting a thorough discussion of such terms as "beautiful," "aesthetic experience," or even "art work." I leave these meanings largely to common sense here. My purpose is only to explore what a realistic epistemology might require of art. It does not require a priori limitation of art to imitation of the real. An excellent art work can be thoroughly unlike anything that occurs in the world and not be intended by the artist to "imitate" (even in Danto's roomy sense) anything. Its substance will still require color, shape, sound, and so on—as do creatures of nature. But the creative reprocessing of form allows for new totalities previously unseen, unthought, and unheard. The more we understand to what extent art and knowledge go in opposite directions, the less we will think that a realistic theory of knowledge must

---

[3]George Santayana, *The Sense of Beauty* (New York: Dover, 1896) 192ff.

[4]Allowing always for the "beautiful" to be mediated by the "unbeautiful" or "ugly"—as in tragedy or gothic romance.

place onerous constraints upon artistic possibilities. Artists, like scientists, "experiment." A scientific experiment is largely evaluated in terms of predictive success, the way it fits reality. An artistic experiment is evaluated in terms of aesthetic success, as an embodiment of beautiful possibilities. Thus, theory construction in science, while creative, intends and is validated by a descriptive or at least pragmatic fit with the world it is about, while artistic creativity requires no such intention or validation.

The notion of knowledge and art going in opposite directions prevents a confining extrapolation from epistemological realism to "artistic realism." It also prevents an extrapolation from creative art to non-foundational epistemology. The problems avoided here are similar to the ones we avoided earlier by distinguishing the autonomous observation framework from the theoretical framework. When these two frameworks were seen as one completely integrated whole, we were faced with a choice between formal foundationalism and the myth of the framework. Either the creativity of theory change ripped observation from its foundations or rigid constructions from observation ruled out theoretical creativity. As long as these two seemed the only alternatives, we were caught by a pendulum swinging back and forth between successive generations of "realists" and "idealists." Giving up on philosophy altogether began to seem more reasonable than further rides on the pendulum. The rise of informal foundationalism as a third alternative showed us a way out. It allowed us to preserve the foundational role of observation without sacrificing theoretical creativity. It allowed "slippage" between the relatively permanent observation framework and the far more volatile domain of theory, so that neither was absorbed or reduced by the other. A similar happy outcome results from an understanding of the "oppositeness" of knowledge and art. The two domains are connected with each other in many mutually enriching ways, but not so closely that either is absorbed or reduced by the other.

What I am calling the "oppositeness" of knowledge and art may seem so evident as to be trivial, but there are other ways to construe the relationship that greatly mitigate the contrast between the two activities. Consider the notion of art as imitation or idealization of the real. Comparison with the phrase "Knowledge is of that which already exists" suggests the rephrasing "Imitation is of that which already exists" and "Idealization is of that which already exists." Knowledge and art are seen as parallel rather than as opposite, with the limitations we have already discussed.

Realists were not the only ones who saw a strong parallel between knowledge and art. Coleridge and Croce were among those who developed a philosophy of art by building upon Kant's notion of "imagination."[5] Perception was understood as the creation of phenomenal objects by the intuitive imagination out of the manifold of sense. Thus perception itself was an activity of art. The making of art-works-properly-so-called was just a freer extension of this fundamental artistic creativity, coupled with a conscious concern for aesthetic results. John Dewey viewed growth in knowledge as the progressive reconstruction of experience.[6] Stimulated by the conflict, confusion, slack, or incoherence of a situation, the intellect reconstructs it so that the result is more determinate, harmonious, and meaningful. A powerful experience of newly created harmony and meaning Dewey called "consummation." Art-properly-so-called is one example of this creative movement from the slack and inchoate to the newly determined and harmonious. Aesthetic experience is one example of the kind of "consummation" that results. What distinguishes fine art from other kinds of human harmonizing is its emphasis upon purely aesthetic results (although for Dewey all forms of consummation have a potential for aesthetic enjoyment). Thus, according to both Croce and Dewey, knowledge is assimilated to the "making of something new" of art. But, as we have seen, this is not necessary for the freedom of art; and, as I have tried to show in earlier chapters, it constitutes an inferior theory of knowledge.

ESOTERIC ART

Most of the heat of arguments among non-philosophers concerning realism in art is generated not by epistemological differences, but by disagreements about the value of certain forms of art. Those who do not appreciate "modern art" frequently appeal to "artistic realism" to justify views that their opponents regard as philistine. Another way to describe this disagreement is the clash between Apollonian and Dionysian or between classical and romantic sensibilities. These distinctions are not exactly to the point, however, because many Dionysian and/or romantic works have

---

[5]Samuel Taylor Coleridge, *Biographia Literaria* (London: Rest Fenner, 1817) Ch. 13-14. Benedetto Croce, *Aesthetic* (New York: Noonday Press, 1953) Ch. 1-2, especially.

[6]See, for example, John Dewey, *Art as Experience* (New York: Minton, Balch, 1934) 35-41, especially.

long since become widely and highly regarded. The real point of the controversy is a shifting demarcation that I shall call "esoteric art."

To understand this term we must recall what I said earlier about the connections between art and other domains. Both the creator of art and the beholder of art bring to their respective activities the multiple conscious and unconscious associations of their lifetimes. Earlier I borrowed Santayana's term "expressiveness" to describe the capacity of an art work to evoke just these kinds of associations in a beholder. An art work can be found expressive by larger or smaller audiences. If it departs far from what most people of artistic interest find familiar and understandable, its audience is likely to be small. If, nevertheless, it is powerfully expressive for a minority of aesthetes, it may be a fine or even great art work.[7] Those who do not find such a work expressive are likely to respond negatively. Since the work does not engage their associations aesthetically, they experience it as a frustration and as an affront. Often they are unwilling to stay with the piece long enough to let its magic work, if it has any. The smaller the group that is able genuinely to appreciate an art work, the more esoteric, by definition, that work is.

Despite its limited audience, esoteric art has an extremely valuable role to play. I mentioned that artists, like scientists, experiment. Esoteric art is at the leading edge of artistic experimentation. Some asethetically successful experiments eventually become popular: the art public finally becomes sufficiently familiar with a piece to allow its expressiveness to work on them. Some esoteric works do not become popular, even though they continue to be well appreciated by an artistic elite. If this elite includes other artists, some of them may find ways to make the experiment more accessible to a wider public, perhaps by

[7]In all of this it is necessary to distinguish between those who genuinely appreciate an art work and those who only wish to appear to do so. An artistic fad results when it becomes "in" to pretend to appreciate certain art works. A fad may attach to works of great or of little merit indifferently. Appeals to artistic realism are frequently made by those who suspect that fads are being perpetrated upon the public and that certain artists are being accorded plaudits and remunerations far beyond their deserts.

incorporating the one-sidedness of an experiment into more inclusive artistic wholes.

My point here is only that a realistic epistemology that acknowledges the oppositeness of knowledge and art is readily able to understand the contributions of esoteric art, despite the frequent use of "realistic" rhetoric to the contrary.

Chapter XII

THE SPECIAL NATURE OF MAN

Our love affair with mathematics has produced a three-headed philosophical offspring: (1) *downward reductionism* or *mechanism,* according to which all is the sum of atomistic parts. The mechanistic project is to spin the seamless mathematical web out of foundational bits and pieces to which all knowledge can be reduced by procedures akin to calculus and geometry. As the connection between the formal atomic foundations and the world waxes problematic, all realism gives way to skeptical forms of phenomenalism. But even in these skeptical forms, it is soon found that in order to save the phenomena, the foundational bits and pieces require a great mixture of mind. And so Father Descartes gives us innate ideas, and even Father Hume turns to psychology to explain causal and other relations.

This mindful gambit gathers strength to produce (2) *upward reductionism* or *idealism,* according to which all is the apparatus of Mind. The idealist project is to show that all apparent differences and even oppositions are just aspects and moments of the dialectical journey of Universal Mind. Here, at least, the temptations to appearance/reality dualism and mind/body dualism, which haunted downward reductionism, are overcome. But, in the end, our well-developed skeptical habits make it hard to accept this Universal Mind and its all-consuming dialectic.

If our hunger for reductionism remains strong, however, we can turn to (3) *sideways reductionism* or *conventionalism,* where all is the function of framework. The project here is to show we can get along better without tying ourselves down to foundations or up to Universal Mind. We simply float sideways on the breezes of convention. As we float along, our philosophical anxieties dissipate in the general ennui. Within each framework we can exercise our mathematical and logical propensities to our fullest humor, but at the framework boundaries we will find no tether but convention. Like clouds of all sizes and shapes, the frameworks come and go, join and separate, without ultimate rhyme or reason—or, if we are sensible, any worry about it.

The often strident rejection of this three-headed offspring has largely been left in the hands of a loose circle of philosophers called "existentialists," who have championed the cause of the individual self and freedom against absorption by the pervasive determinations of one-dimensional philosophical systems. Anyone who has been with me through the preceding eleven chapters can guess I have much sympathy for the existentialists as critics of the recent tradition. But, as we shall see in this chapter, existentialists are caught in the web of that which they attack.

First we shall examine some of the themes of the existentialist revolt. Afterward, I shall close the chapter with some brief remarks about the special nature of man as suggested by informal foundationalism.

1. *The notion of a conceptual scheme—and of being inside or outside it.* Kierkegaard, Heidegger, Sartre, Jaspers, and other existentialists understand "conceptual scheme" as a formal mathematical/logical system.[1] All parts of the scheme are defined and understood in terms of necessary logical connections with other parts of the scheme as a whole. The very nature of a conceptual scheme shows, they believe, that individual existence cannot be caught in its net. We must strive mightily, says Heidegger in *Being and Time,* to avoid becoming so obsessed with "beings" (individuals as construed by conceptual schemes) that

---

[1]Examples abound, but the following references will serve as an initial guide: Søren Kierkegaard, *Concluding Unscientific Postscript* (Princeton: Princeton University Press, 1941) 99-133; Jean-Paul Sartre, "The Root of the Chesnut Tree," in his *Nausea* (Norfolk CT: New Directions, 1964). For a more standardly philosophical formulation of the same point, see Jean-Paul Sartre, *Being and Nothingness* (New York: Philosophical Library, 1956). Karl Jaspers, *Philosophy,* 3 vols. (Chicago: University of Chicago Press, 1969) 1:226-49. Jaspers criticizes the reductivism of both positivism and idealism. He also discusses objective and subjective being, ibid., 47ff. Martin Heidegger, *Being and Time* (New York: Harper, 1962) especially the "Introduction."

we neglect or forget "Being." "Being," it appears, is the name Heidegger gives to that realm which radically eludes our conceptual schemes—primal existence as opposed to what we take things to be. Sartre describes this realm that escapes our schemes as "*de trop,*" literally "too much."[2] It is too much for our conceptual schemes to handle. It always threatens to burst the conceptual bounds and upset the order our consciousness imposes. This is what Sartre means when he says that existence is "absurd": it is not logical, it is not mathematical. Our conceptual schemes codify our expectations, just as Hume told us our notions of cause and effect do, but there is absolutely nothing to keep existence from crossing us up at any time.

Existentialist aversion for the view that conceptual-schemes-tell-all applies not only to idealist and mechanist schemes, but also to conventionalist schemes. Indeed, Kierkegaard, Nietzsche, Sartre, Jaspers, Arendt, and others reserve their strongest diatribes for people living "in the mass" or in stereotyped roles.[3] Nietzsche's much admired *Uebermensch* is utterly himself—freely exploding the shackles of convention, creating himself in a way that anticipates Sartre's notion of freedom. Nothing eludes the conceptual scheme more completely than the self.

All existentialists reject God as the Great-Thinker-of-the-Great-Conceptual-Scheme. But Pascal, Kierkegaard, Jaspers, Marcel, Dostoyevski, and others retrieve God as the one who is most ultimately beyond our conceptual schemes, who speaks to us in surprising and soul-searching ways, and whom we believe, not out of necessity, but from choice and from freely given trust. By the standards of the conceptual schemes, such belief is absurd—and this is precisely what recommends it to the anti-schematic existentialist mind. *Credo quia absurdum:* Tertullian's slogan captures the beyond-rational rationale exactly.

A central problem for existentialism is that it takes its notion of "conceptual scheme" from the three-headed philosophical off-

---

[2]Sartre, "The Root of the Chesnut Tree."

[3]In addition to the earlier citations, see Karl Jaspers, *Man in the Modern Age* (London: George Routledge and Sons, 1933) especially 104; Søren Kierkegaard, *Works of Love* (Princeton: Princeton University Press, 1946) and *The Present Age* (New York: Oxford University Press, 1940); Friedrich Nietzsche, *The Philosophy of Nietzsche* (New York: Modern Library, 1965) 126-27 (from *Thus Spake Zarathustra*) 135-36, 200-204 (from *Beyond Good and Evil*) 133ff. (from *Ecce Homo*); Hannah Arendt, *The Human Condition* (Chicago: University of Chicago Press, 1958) especially chapter 2.

spring of mathematics. It then observes that there is much of great importance that cannot be captured by this notion. And so various existentialists introduce additional and supposedly unschematic domains: Pascal's domain of the heart, Kierkegaard's individual existence, Heidegger's Being, Sartre's absurd, Neitzsche's creativity, and the exhilarating yet weighty burden of freedom carried by them all. The result is not a repudiation of mathematics, science, or conceptual schemes, but rather a new version of dualism. Conceptual schemes are fine as far as they go; but, of course, they cannot capture individual existence, Being, pure consciousness, and so on. The existentialist dualisms, like most dualisms, are problematic. How is it that existentialists are able to talk at such great length about these domains beyond conceptual schemes? Does not their doing so require the use of a conceptual scheme? And if they are trying to talk about that which cannot be conceptualized, are they not giving us another unknowable thing-in-itself, with all its attendant contradictions—long since exploded by Hegel and others?

The connection between existentialism and Kant, while not so simple as these questions would imply, is nevertheless of great importance. The writings of Schopenhauer and Nietzsche sound a transformed Kantian theme that is carried forward by Heidegger, Sartre, Camus, and others. Schopenhauer accepts Kant's distinction between the phenomena and the thing-itself.[4] He denies, however, that the thing-itself is unknowable—thus avoiding the contradiction of having things to say about the unknowable. He calls the thing-itself "will." For Schopenhauer this will is a blind, striving desire, full of suffering because ungratifiable. It is the radical positive evil of the universe, in the throes of which goodness is a mere negation achieved by various forms of aesthetic contemplation. In his early and very Schopenhauerian work,[5] Nietzsche describes this aesthetic "redemption" as a resolution of metaphysical conflict in the domain of artistic illusion, a resolution that leaves the underlying conflict untouched, but is nevertheless a worthy achievement—all that can be hoped for. These "creative" and "aesthetic" preoccupations of Schopenhauer and Nietzsche

---

[4]Arthur Schopenhauer, *The World as Will and Idea* (London: K. Paul, Trench, 1909).

[5]Friedrich Nietzsche, *The Birth of Tragedy from the Spirit of Music* (Garden City NY: Doubleday Anchor, 1956).

carry over into the work of later existentialists. Even more fundamental, however, is the notion of the "thing-itself" as absolutely "irrational." Its "irrationality" is a function of its contrast with the phenomenon. The phenomenon is the rational organization of the thing-itself into *individuals* that *causally* interact with one another. Individuation and causal necessity are the linchpins of rationality. The thing-itself, by contrast, is undifferentiated and unnecessitated. Both Schopenhauer and Nietzsche believe that we have experiential intimations of the thing-itself, perceptions of orgiastic oneness, vertiginous disorientation, or the horrible abyss of chaos. Sartre will later say that these experiential intimations are more a matter of feeling than of knowing.

The contrast between existentialism and Hegelian idealism as two lines of development from Kant is clear. Hegel drops the unknowable thing-itself and makes mind (and thereby rationality) the fundamental metaphysical reality. Existentialists make the thing-itself fundamental, but understand it as knowably irrational. *Phenomenal* experience is the domain of rationality, where reason imposes individuation and causality.

Existentialists see the three forms of reductionism as three ways of losing truthful and vital contact with the thing-itself. Highly organized reductive schemata are for them clearly the products of the phenomenal enterprise. When these schemata are seen as potentially including all that we can be aware of, or even all that is, they push aside consciousness of the thing-itself. This, perhaps cowardly, untruthfulness keeps its adherents from addressing the fundamental questions of existence. Only by bravely facing the irrational abyss of the thing-itself is "redemption" possible—either by a leap of faith in God (Kierkegaard and others) or by aesthetic revolt and artistic creativity (Schopenhauer, Nietzsche, Heidegger, Sartre, and others). The latter form of "redemption" is, of course, very limited: it leaves the fundamental irrationality (absurdity) untouched; somehow the aesthetic solution is nevertheless regarded as better than no solution. This last intuition has brought against such existentialists the charge that, despite their vaunted bravery, they too are untruthful in the end.

To the informal foundationalist, this existentialist form of realism, despite its moments of great power and insight, remains, on the whole, clumsy. Its clumsiness is a function of its radical adherence to Kant's bifurcation of reality into the phenomenon and the thing-itself. For the existentialist this bifurcation does not split the known from the unknown, but rather the rational from the irrational. The rationality of the phenomena is for the existentialist a function of reason (understanding) that structures phenomena according to its own principles (for example, the principles of individuation and of causality).

Informal foundationalism avoids this bifurcation of the rational and the thing-itself. It too emphasizes the fundamental importance of nonconceptual or preconceptual awareness, but claims that preconceptual awareness is awareness of a structured world full of individuals and of causal relations. In other words, things-themselves include individuals (such as trees and cats) that causally interact. We develop our concepts for these individual things and for the causal relations between them from our awareness of them and of their causal relations. Individuality and causality are not imposed by the understanding; they characterize things-themselves. In earlier chapters I have argued that this view resuscitates givenness and shows how knowledge can have foundations.

Granted that, for the informal foundationalist, things-themselves are to this extent rational, they are, nevertheless, to a great extent "irrational" as well. Reductive strategies have not succeeded. Nor is there even momentum toward success, despite our advances. The drive toward a unified field theory in physics, for example, is based upon the Big Bang theory of the universe's origin—which, because it in principle defies analysis of its causes, epitomizes irrationality, from the human point of view, at the heart of the physical order. The notion has long since dawned that, as our understanding of the world progresses, gaps in our knowledge *multiply*. It seems likely that we can never catch up with the outer limits of the expanding universe, either literally or rationally. In the name of rationality, Albert Einstein refused to accept the indeterminacies of quantum theory; but in the end his very resistance, given the evidence, appeared less than rational. We *do* need an epistemological dualism between the known and the unknown/unknowable; but do we need a metaphysical dualism between the rational phenomena and the irrational thing-itself?

Why cannot the things-themselves be seen as complex enough to be both understandable up to a point, and yet not *fully* comprehensible? The answer that comes to mind is the loud echo of Descartes: the comprehensible and incomprehensible cannot be part of the same ontological domain because they are not reducible to one another! (Remember how Descartes set out to divide the universe into two domains: the one analyzable by mechanics—the material, primary qualities—and the other, not so analyzable—the mental, including secondary, qualities.) But if this is the assumption that governs the existentialist phenomena/things-themselves dualism, we can see that existentialism is trapped in the nets of that which it would criticize. On the one hand, existentialists plead the cause of the irrational or super-rational against thoroughgoing mechanical and mathematical systems. On the other hand, they do so in terms of a distinction between phenomena and things-themselves, a distinction based on the ironclad rules for just such thoroughgoing mechanical and mathematical systems.

Informal foundationalism avoids more successfully the traps set by the love affair with mathematics; this has the further advantage of resolving the antinomy that results from postulating a noumenal consciousness and a phenomenal world, from making consciousness so special that there seems no valid way to talk about it. Once trees and horses are seen as more than phenomenal objects constituted by consciousness, we avoid what seems to be an unbridgeable Kantian split between the phenomenal world and noumenal consciousness. The trees and horses are as real and as much things-themselves as consciousness is. When we analyze intentional states and intentional language, we do not arrive at intentional, understood as merely phenomenal, objects. Intentional states and intentional language can be about things-themselves, whether trees, horses, or consciousness. This has the effect of locating consciousness in the world. It is, therefore, not, as Sartre thinks, the negation of the world—as that which constitutes the world while not being constituted by it in turn.[6] Consciousness is *of* the world, but it does not constitute the world.

Finally, informal foundationalism upgrades other people from the status of phenomenal objects constituted by my consciousness of them to individual existences presupposed by my consciousness of them.[7] Another human being is as much a locus of individual existence and consciousness as I myself am. It is true that I have a different perspective on myself than others do—I am able to introspect my state of mind. But once I acknowledge oth-

---

[6]Jean-Paul Sartre, *Being and Nothingness.*

[7]Cf. Jean-Paul Sartre, "The Existence of the Other," ibid., where he discusses the inevitable conflict that exists between people, who must see one another as objects.

ers as having individual existence, I can be open to the evidence that they have the same powers of introspection I have. Once I understand this, epistemological ground is laid for the moral tenet that I ought neither to treat others as mere objects nor let myself be so treated. For the informal foundationalist, there is no contradiction of epistemological necessities in this moral principle.

2. *The notion of determinism—and of being or not being free.* To understand the absolute centrality of extreme views of human freedom in existentialist thought, one must first understand how existentialists see determinism. Determinism is a notion governed by the concepts of cause, effect, and necessity. These concepts together form part of a conceptual scheme that rules our perception of objects in the world. But as we have already seen in (1) above, existentialists insist that pure consciousness is neither an object in the world nor ruled by any conceptual scheme whatever. Therefore, causality and necessity do not apply to pure consciousness, *pour soi, Existenz,* or whatever one calls the noumenal self. But that which causality does not rule is free, utterly free. This is true even though it is common for the self to renounce this freedom and let itself be ruled by others or by convention. But even such renunciation of freedom—morally/aesthetically destitute, so we are told, as it is—expresses the radical freedom of the self to choose slavery; for even "not to choose is to choose." It is for precisely these reasons that existentialists hold freedom to be the nature of the self. Freedom is absolutely pervasive in the acts of the self. If one acts according to a standard or to follow set rules, it is only because one has first chosen the standard or chosen the rules. And if one is simply ruled by the conventions that surround him, he has, however uncreatively, chosen to be ruled by them.

Informal foundationalism, on the contrary, argues that conceptual schemes can refer to things-themselves through the autonomous observation framework, which is built up in the first place by means of preconceptual awareness of things-themselves. Therefore, it does not follow that because the notion of causal necessity is part of a conceptual scheme, it cannot be applied to things-themselves. On the contrary, the rocks and planets to which we so readily apply the notion are as real as the noumenal self.

I said earlier that informal foundationalism does not deny human free will. It does deny that there are a priori grounds for saying that humans are free—as existentialists insist. Nor are there a priori grounds for saying humans are not free, as an airtight mechanistic view of the-world-including-man might insist. The question cannot be decided on the basis of airtight conceptual schemes that are thought either to apply en masse or to apply not at all to humans. It requires creative insight into human behavior, including one's own. My own primary insight is that I am frequently able to decide which of a number of alternative motives will determine my actions, that I am frequently able to do otherwise than I do. Others seem to have the same capacity. No argument for determinism has been able to shake my confidence in this insight and in moral reasoning and political institutions based upon it. Arguments for determinism derive from megalithic confidence in extrapolating conceptual schemes (in this case, the mechanistic one) beyond the bounds of evidence. The desire to do this is part of the heady feeling that constitutes the love affair with mathematics. Having based an acceptance of human freedom on a posteriori grounds, I am ready to accept much that existentialists say about the importance of "responsibility." It seems to me that this notion should be part of any thorough and sound morality.

Before concluding this chapter, I would like to make some further remarks about the special nature of man as seen from the vantage point of informal foundationalism. A central reason for the success of informal foundationalism is its view of the connection between the autonomous observation framework and the theoretical framework. Theories are attempts at creative insight into the underlying causes and explanations of that which observation presents. The positing of theories is not an exercise in mathematical or logical derivation. It seems, then, that our first conclusion about man is that he has a mind capable of creative insight, a mind capable of arriving at useful and even truthful conclusions by procedures not reducible to logical or mathematical steps.

This capacity for creative insight, it seems to me, is more clearly a unique property of the human mind than is the capacity to wield universals. Primary examples of such universals from Pythagoras to the present have been mathematical universals. Yet computers appear to wield these universals with great aplomb. Computers are not, however, capable of creative insight. All examples of artificial intelligence are concatenations at lightning speed of extremely simple mathematical or logical steps. Every centimeter of the speedy journey is under complete logical control. Computers have been programmed to play backgammon at the highest level of competition. They can perform as well as any human. But no computer has yet been programmed to play chess at the highest level. The best chess champions can beat any computer. The reason is that chess is too complex for computer-style calculations to handle. A computer decides what move to make by first playing out all the consequences of all the available moves to see which one brings the optimum results. Chess has too many possibilities for a computer to compute. Backgammon does not.

Humans, on the other hand, are able, without mentally playing out all possibilities, to "intuit" superior moves. Computers cannot keep pace with the intuitive shortcuts of the human mind in matters of vast complexity. I am not predicting that no computer will ever be successfully programmed as a world champion chess player. My point is that such a computer's mastery will be no more than a bigger version of typical computer activity: the lightning-fast concatenation of simpleminded and uninsightful logical/mathematical steps on a massive scale.

What I am suggesting is that computers will never be able to duplicate the creative capacities of the human mind. Computers can be programmed to think in only mathematically reductive ways. If reductionism were true of the world and of the human mind, computers could, in principle, eventually do everything that minds can do and do it better. Informal foundationalism argues that reductionism is not true of world and mind. It seems a contradiction in terms to program a computer to think creatively. A computer cannot get outside its program. It is a creature entirely of logical/mathematical necessities. Informal foundationalism insists that theoretical activity takes one beyond the confines of mathematical/logical calculation and derivation.

Can we be certain that no electronic device will ever be able to step outside its program? Perhaps not. But if by some miraculous accident one ever does, it will embody "immateriality" in the same sense that humans embody it—by creative thought and freedom of action. It will have slipped the mathematical paradigm that gave it birth. What sort of plan would we follow to make such a creature? We seem to be asking if we can make something, the making of which contradicts the meaning of human technology. Such creation seems more likely in biological science than in computer science. But, then, the biological sciences copy and rearrange life as we find it. Any intelligent life produced this way will be no more than a variation on the kind of intelligence we already have.

When we look around at the buildings, libraries, technologies, scientific systems, works of art, and expressions of philosophical and religious understanding that surround us, we are seeing the products of the human capacity for "creative insight." No other species of the animal kingdom shows capacities that more than very distantly resemble the human sources of civilization. "Artificial intelligence" is itself a product of human creative insight and a tool for its further exercise. It is not a locus of such insight, however; nor are there grounds for expecting it to become such. Confident expectations to the contrary, it seems to me, are based on a faulty understanding of what computers actually do and/or a lack of appreciation of what humans do. Despite our tendency to anthropomorphize our surroundings—often we have attributed human qualities to nature, now we attribute them to machines—all the evidence indicates that man has no competitor on earth but himself.

CONCLUSION

If the argument of this book has been cogent, here are some of its highlights:

(1) The attack on givenness did not succeed.
(2) The observation framework allows for observational knowledge to develop autonomously, that is, without logically prior connection with any philosophical or scientific theory.
(3) The autonomous development of the observation framework is made possible by its connection with preconceptual awareness of an already structured world.
(4) The autonomy of the observation framework makes it a steady foundational reference point for changing theories.
(5) An understanding of "explaphors" shows that the penetration of observational contexts by theoretical terms does not reduce the autonomy of the observation framework.
(6) The passage from observational foundations to theoretical explanations is not reducible to logical steps. Since this process (I call it "creative insight") is not merely logical, it can be exemplified, but not fully analyzed.
(7) "Creative insight" in science aims for explanations that are true, but usually lacks sufficient evidence for more than pragmatic success. The latter, pace pragmatism, is a necessary, but not sufficient, condition for truth. (See 11 below.)
(8) Very strong truth claims for some explanations resulting from creative insight can at times be justified. In both science and metaphysics, the requirements for such strong truth claims are strenuous.
(9) The myth of the framework is not needed:
    (a) to overcome skepticism (appearance/reality dualism),
    (b) to overcome mind/body dualism,
    (c) to justify political toleration,
    (d) to allow for artistic freedom.

    Informal foundationalism does these things as well.

(10) Informal foundationalism is not vulnerable to the attacks upon formal foundationalism made by the myth of the framework.
(11) Pragmatism (the justification procedure often used by the myth of the framework) works less well than informal foundationalism. This defeats pragmatism on its own ground.
(12) Skeptical conventionalism manifests inherent contradictions that make it an unfit instrument for passing on the traditions of a culture to the next generation.
(13) "Creative insight" suggests a non-reductive view of the world in general and of human nature in particular.

My purpose has not been to defend philosophy's position or importance as a field of study. I have let the chips fall where they might on this issue. Realism does not require philosophy to instruct scientists that they are studying things-themselves rather than phenomena. Only philosophy would have made them think otherwise in the first place. The wispy picture of reality presented by phenomenalists was rarely accepted by scientists, who (rightly) felt they were wrestling with being of much greater thickness. Given my criticisms of many philosophical views, I could not credibly recommend that, as a general rule, scientists, theologians, artists, and technicians defer to philosophers.

But philosophy is inevitable, nevertheless. It seems we cannot repress the human thirst for deeper understanding. But is this thirst just a symptom of absurdity?

Not if informal foundationalism is right.

INDEX